The ABC's of Apostleship Book 2

Discipling Apostolic Christians

A Congregational Discipleship Study Guide

By Paula A. Price, PhD

All scripture used in this publication is taken from the King James, ISV, & New King James Versions of the Holy Bible unless otherwise specified.

ABC's of Apostleship 2: Discipling Apostolic Christians
A Discipleship Study Guide

PPM Global Resources, Inc.

Tulsa, Oklahoma 74136

ISBN 1-886288-17-8

Contents

Preface
Apostolic Discipleship

Church leaders, as you introduce Discipling Apostolic Christians to your membership, keep in mind that its content is very new to the wider body of Christ. Understanding Jesus as an apostle is foreign to the majority of His congregations. So, it will take many of them a while to come to grips with this side of His divine offices. His modern ecclesia does not know its Savior apostolically. It has not heard His word from the perspective of those who delivered the New Testament's full gospel to the world. Of which, by the way, there are nearly two dozen strains to preach and teach.

The majority of the body of Christ is only acquainted with the gospel of their salvation. This statement is made based on the well-known lack of scripture knowledge among the contemporary members of the Lord's body. Also, it is made in light of the overwhelming New Testament only congregations that have no sense of the contribution the Old Testament scriptures made to it. Consequently, 21st century Christianity only knows Jesus the Messiah evangelically. It sees Him as little more than the Son of God who came to save the world from its sin. Not innately wrong, this limited view of the Lord's earthly ministry paints a much too narrow a picture of what the Sovereign of creation really incarnated and came to earth to achieve.

Apostolic Christians are distinct because they know that there is a great deal more to learn about the Lord of glory than what is popularized today. You as a member of this training class will tap into all that Jesus came to do. As you advance in your study, you will get a rare peek into the Savior that you have loved and served for years. Unit after unit brings you face to face with our amazing God and His Redeemer to baptize you into Apostolic Christianity, the Godhead's vision for a good portion of the modern church worldwide.

All of this is to say that pastors and trainers should realize the jolting power of this material. Expect that in some instances it will initially stun some of your people. To counteract this reaction, your apostolic discipleship program should be taught in small segments for your learners to digest it well. Lesson plans should cover no more than one or two topics in a single session. Time should be set aside for extensive discussions to allow God's people to process what they learn and adapt to the new world being unveiled to them. Make every effort to see that the entire church takes in the information properly and keeps up. To this end, practice activities should be plentiful, fun, and unpressured.

As said earlier, for many people thinking about the Lord apostolically rather than evangelically is completely new. Since all new things have the potential to be unsettling at times, presenting the Lord in this manner calls for a fresh way of teaching and learning what will take a while to sink in. Familiarizing today's church with this side of God will involve some work, so be patient. Expect to set aside at least a year to walk your congregations and ministers through this unique discipleship track. Along the way, encourage them to embrace and absorb it, bit-by-bit. Ease them into it by breaking up the study periodically to explore their issues and reactions to it. Respond to their concerns and difficulties in the moment as much as possible. Realize that every discipleship program is a marathon not a sprint, so give it the time it takes to get your people comfortable with becoming Apostolic Christians. That means allowing them to question, challenge, and act out what they learn in class, in order to get used to this new mind of Christianity. To facilitate this, create a peaceful but definitely productive environment to help them do so. Just do not rush it.

Take Your Time

As a discipler of Apostolic Christians, you definitely want to avoid jumping around the book. Go through it unit by unit so that there are no gaps in your people's comprehension, or retention. That is the only way they will convert to apostleship transformed and not just rollover into it deformed. As you go through it, stop and do the exercises with them. Do not skip an activity because you as the trainer understand it. What is more important is that your people get it too so they can readily shift to apostleship with you. In addition, make as many opportunities as you can for them to do the assignments: separate them into teams or small groups; and establish a buddy system among your people that motivates all learners to work with one another.

Lastly, include your entire organization in this discipleship program to reduce fractures and panic flights. Contain and manage the understandable dread associated with the unknown by enlightening everyone in your congregation at the same time, all the way down to your youth. After all, you do want them all to become Apostolic Christians, and not shun it out of fear and confusion. Adjust the material as needed to each group's level of knowledge and learning ability. As a final exhortation, let me say again, <u>do not rush the process.</u>

Discipling Apostolic Christians should be a marathon, not a sprint. I could go so far as to say that for some of your learners, it could be a slow cruise. Learning and changing takes time because human beings grow slowly; so let them enjoy the journey with you. Here is the first of the many apostleship definitives you will learn in this program.

How to Use This Guide

Discipling Apostolic Christians seeks to help apostles or apostolic ministers transform their traditional or classic Christian ministries into apostolic ones, beginning with discipling the people to take part in it with you. Therefore, it recommends that entire congregations be completely immersed in it, starting with the kingdom's leadership and staff. Why, you ask? The answer is because apostleship does not just happen to the leader that is becoming an apostle, but it also happens to the whole church, business or ministry. Everyone affected by the apostle's emergence and/or rise to God's service must be transitioned to this ministry emphasis from the inside out, something

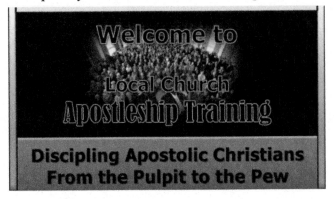

that this guide will do for you. When a leader becomes an apostle, their whole organization becomes apostolic. That is why this study's sound and pointed information especially targets the missing link between how apostleship was initiated, established, and functions today. It recognizes that the people with the new apostles require discipleship to go to the next level as a maturing institution.

While it has seen some success, the truth is apostleship should have made infinitely more progress than it has so far. There are many reasons for its slow pace, but a main one I discerned is that it mostly left its people (disciples) behind. Those to take apostleship to the world do not as yet know exactly what it is. With so little congregational material available to equip them, most of those shifting to it today simply enjoy the apostles in their lives as a novelty, not as instruments of a full-scale metamorphosis of their Christian faith.

Only dabbling in it from time to time, a number of those passing through its gates give little thought to getting deeply involved in the apostleship that scripture presents. For example, the idea of going from being evangelical to apostolic has never really taken hold of them. For these and other reasons, apostleship for the most part has focused mainly on the apostles, leaving God's flock standing off to the side admiring their efforts. The distance between the apostles and those embracing them is evident from how the majority of God's body continues to grope for answers to the mantle and its ministry.

As it stands now, only a few modern Christians connect with this critically needed foundational New Testament ministry. That must change  drastically for the Lord's will to be done in His church and kingdom. Presently, only a handful of the Lord's people can relate to the apostles they meet. The fullness of what apostleship brings to those that accept them lingers in the background. For instance, although the apostles lead and people support their efforts, neither side adequately furnishes the other with the tangible values hidden in this office. That is what Discipling Apostolic Christians aims to rectify. This book provides a study guide for church Bible classes, leadership trainings, midweek services, and special group development. Here is some advice you should follow as you introduce and present this material to your flocks.

1. Train everyone at their particular level.
2. Learn it well yourself before training others.
3. Training leaders closest to the transiting apostle first
4. Teach leaders to train those beneath them
5. Make it fun
6. Adapt it to your vision

There is more that you will see as you go along. These tips are given to make sure you start out right so that you end up right where you want to be, taking your people with you.

Training Knowledge To Be Gained

What You Will Learn

1. Why You Need This Information
2. Apostles as Revelators
3. Jesus' Kingship and Kingdom
4. Christians' Superior Premise
5. Heaven on Earth
6. The Christian Genus
7. Secrets From the Foundation of the World
8. Living the Godhead's Life
9. Exemplifying Your Hereditary Heritage
10. How Christianity Became the Almighty's First Civilization
11. How to Avoid Apostasy
12. Christianity as a Nation Not a Religion
13. What Jesus is Doing Now
14. Wrapping Up This World's Ages

Introduction

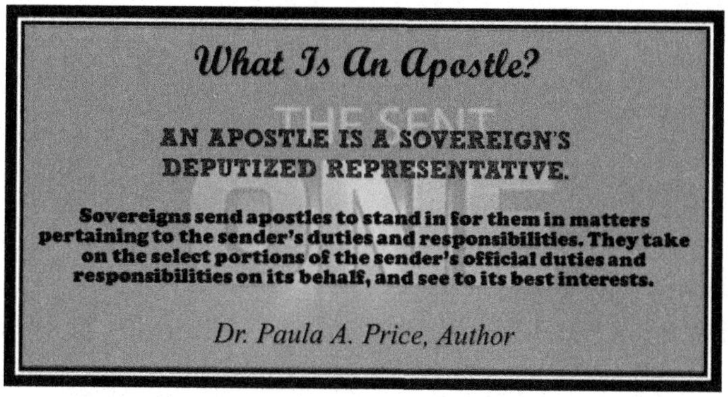

What Is An Apostle?

AN APOSTLE IS A SOVEREIGN'S DEPUTIZED REPRESENTATIVE.

Sovereigns send apostles to stand in for them in matters pertaining to the sender's duties and responsibilities. They take on the select portions of the sender's official duties and responsibilities on its behalf, and see to its best interests.

Dr. Paula A. Price, Author

The ABC's of Apostleship 2: Shifting Focus

As Book 2 of your ABC's of Apostleship training, this study sets aright the church's historical foundations by focusing on apostles' disciples, their audiences and targets, not just on the apostles themselves. This training may well be hailed by some modern apostles and prophets as the missing link to apostleship's wide scale reinstatement. The link that is missing is the discipleship of Apostolic Christians. It is essential because early apostolic attention stressed identifying, strengthening, and esteeming the apostles, while overlooking the discipleship of those to become part of their commissions.

The New Era Apostleship Discipleship Way

To Disciple Apostolic Christians

1. *Empower the Apostles*
2. *Orientate Their Teams*
3. *Disciple Their Converts*
4. *Transform Their Works*

Understandably though nonetheless unfortunate, the apostle's commission team and congregations got lost in God's revival of apostleship in the contemporary church. Initial reinstatement efforts concentrated too little on those to take (and explain apostleship to the everyday world), and too much on the rank and authority of the apostle. That oversight created an alienating gap between the apostles and their disciples, with those ordained to their work

being too confused or skeptical to shift from their evangelical roots.

Designed to shift the 21st century church to New Era Apostleship, this training will move those who are chosen from evangelicalism to apostleship (**if** that is God's will for them). Those feeling the tug of the new, who are ready to migrate from the old, will find this process invigorating and arming, which admittedly is not for everyone that is saved by Christ Jesus. To those who are called to it, this work promises to bring apostleship its long overdue kingdom dignity and to motivate believers to cooperate with what the Lord has been pushing for the last several decades, which is the full reinstatement of apostleship over His church. Discipling Apostolic Christians is important because after all, without the people, like every other endeavor, apostleship is empty. It takes apostles making disciples after their own kind to validate the office. Reproducing themselves is the best way for apostles to staff and support their commissions. Going through this material and completing its exercises goes a long way toward achieving that end. This congregational training will convert a non-apostolic church to apostleship intelligently and seamlessly because all elements of the ministry will be transformed at the same time. Using Discipling Apostolic Christians as a conversion tool will produce the same type of Apostolic Christian throughout God's kingdom that defined His early church.

Over time, you will find yourself becoming more and more like the Christians they were. Completing this study guide will bring you in deeper touch with the Lord Jesus Christ as Sovereign <u>and</u> Savior than you have ever before. Its activities, tasks, and exercises will enable you to transform into an Apostolic Christian and take up your part of His New Era Apostleship™ Restitution campaign. Other benefits to be gained from this training's success are the swift spreading of the term "Apostolic Christian" and rapid conversion of appointed contemporary Christians to apostleship. Your intelligence and enthusiasm will inspire others to find their unique place in Christ and jump onboard His awesome restitution campaign. These make up the main initiatives of New Era Apostleship™ Restitution. So read on, finish your training, and then go make Apostolic Christians lots and lots of them!

Biblically Sound Apostolic Christians

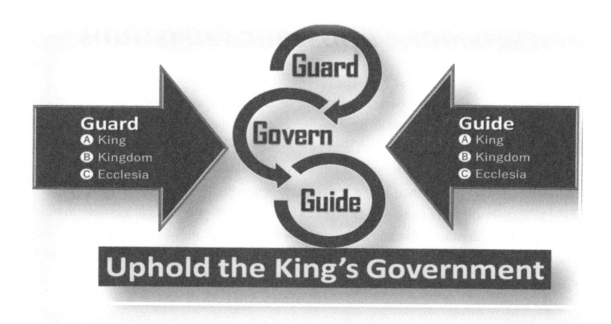

UNIT 1

The Purpose of This Teaching:
To Make Apostolic Christians

Did you know that you are right now, today an Apostolic Christian? Well it is true. If you are born again in Christ Jesus, according to the word of God, you not only became a Christian, you became an apostolic one as well. While it may be that you eventually joined this or that church or doctrinal camp after you were saved, in reality, none of it matters because all Christians begin their life in Jesus Christ apostolically. For those of you who are called by God to apostleship, this work will strengthen you. From it, you will get answers to quite a few of those nagging questions about apostles' works that mystify and deter people from joining or staying with them. I am talking about questions like why so many of their works remain small in size, have meager economies, and seem unstable when the word and power of God is clearly evident in them.

This training guide is for all apostolic ministers and leaders, no matter what area of the fivefold you serve. Taking your disciples through apostleship training could be just what they need to buy into your commission and become 21st century Apostolic Christians. Whenever believers say they want to return to the days of the early church, they are unknowingly talking about going back to its foundation, which is apostleship. All Christ's offspring were conceived in the womb of apostles and entered the world through the birth canal of apostleship. That is how we begin and it is the only way the church Jesus Christ evenisioned will continue to be His. That means not just affirming it belongs to Him as its founder, but moreso seeing that it remains under His direct domination. Therefore, making apostolic disciples, or disciples of apostleship, is the only way to stabilize and expand the numerous apostolic commissions the Lord Jesus is handing out in this era. Here is why. As shocking as it may be to those who discredit and reject apostles, the preceding declaration is the absolute truth. All who are born again in Jesus Christ entered His body apostolically. The implications of this fact, though staggering, must be examined and accepted if apostleship is to be taken seriously and those called to it are to feel secure enough to get behind it. Unless something credible tells people that apostleship is safe, they will continue to eye it warily and hesitate to join and support it. So let us get to the heart of the matter; beginning with apostleship's origins and history, which requires going all the way back to eternity, where everything began.

The first Christians ever to be born on earth were apostolic, and Christianity being rooted in God's first civilization in heaven is what made it so. The idea of God's first civilization is covered more later in the book. For now, you only need to see Christianity and apostleship as eternal and not temporal the way everything else in this world is. Both began and will prevail throughout eternity as a result. For this reason, under Jesus' reign, all sectarian and denominational views on Christianity and their divisions will give way to apostleship in heaven. The Savior alludes to this in Matthew 19:28 and Luke 22:28-30. So let's dig into this a little deeper.

ACTS 26:18

"To open their eyes, in order to turn them from darkness to light, and from the power of Satan to God, that they may receive forgiveness of sins and an inheritance among those who are sanctified by faith that is in Me."

What you are about to learn here will empower those ordained by God to populate God's kingdom apostolically, to participate in His imposing apostolic era. When you do become completely apostolic in your Christianity, you will feel good about it and see it as the next logical progression in your Christian walk. As you read on, this will all make better sense to you.

Many people believing and backing apostles today are still too disconnected with the office to appreciate why it exists. When their loved ones question them about apostleship, most apostolic followers dodge the question because they are uneasy about the answers to them. Others defensively shutdown when asked about apostleship because they feel too ill equipped to explain to others the

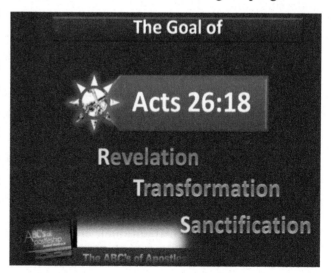

The Goal of

Acts 26:18

Revelation

Transformation

Sanctification

differences apostles make in their lives. Deeply confused souls simply downplay its advantages or sidestep the subject altogether. Far too many apostolic converts, despite their fervency, lack the words to tell their family and friends the type of church they attend or its benefits. Often they cannot say with conviction the advantages of having apostles as their spiritual leaders.

The wisdom of this book will help you who experience these discomforts immensely by giving language and insight into what you know in your heart to be the will of God for you. By the end of your training you will be able to respond bravely to apostolic issues and questions in the future.

Where Apostleship Stands Today

As it stands now, many apostles' followers remain evangelicals that merely visit apostolic meetings. Most of them only refresh themselves in God's apostolic pools now and again. Very few of them give any real thought to understanding apostleship enough to embrace it, let alone seriously consider it as the next step in their Christian walk. Despite how long apostleship has been around; numerous apostolic seekers fail to relate it to traditional Christianity. For instance, only a handful of them know that Apostolic Christians are the first converts to Jesus Christ.

Countless modern believers doctrinally talked into rejecting apostles are unaware that they are who birthed and shepherded the early church. Unfortunately, modern apostles reinforced the errant notions about their validity when they assert that apostles should not pastor, or be tied to a local church. That contention conflicts with scripture although it is understandable how the conclusion came to be. The truth has been withheld from Christ's church for centuries

Apostles Are:

1) Commissioned to Discharge an Office
2) Sent With a Kingdom Message
3) Deputized to Represent, Manifest, Reflect the Lord Jesus Christ
4) Delegated Authority to Legislate in Christ's Stead
5) Dispatched to a Territory
6) Endued With Power
7) Impacted with Miracles, Signs & Wonders
8) Bestowed a Dispensation
9) Assigned a Sphere of Ambassadorship
10) Set 1st Over the Lord's New Creation Church
11) Endowed with a Body of Mysteries to Steward
12) Accredited by Jesus Christ as His Ambassadors

and now it is time for it to come forth. That is the only way today's Christian can get the answers to their questions about what apostles can add to their spiritual life. You might be asking at this point how we got here, or what power or action decreed that apostles were no more. You may also be wondering how apostles became obsolete, while the other officers of the church (minus the prophets) were popularized. For instance, contemporary prophets then and now seem to be viewed as less credible than the apostles are, except for those in scripture.

One answer to apostles' traditional, and maybe theological, disrepute is found in the Vatican II Dogmatic Constitution of Divine Revelation. Briefly, it decreed that apostles were no longer necessary because the church was born and the bishops were to take over. Essentially, when you hear the phrase "Apostolic Succession", this is what is meant. The term and its procedures are the displacement ideology that de-canonized apostleship although it birthed the church, contending that the founding office of God's kingdom and church died out and appointed the bishops to assume their roles. So when you hear the phrase in the future, know that it maintains apostles gave way to bishops, despite the office never being abolished in scripture. No one has ever been able to say how or when God replaced apostleship with the bishopric. Yet stubbornly, the error has been (and continues to be) shoveled as a divine edict with nothing more supporting it than the "will of man". Although no sacred text today proves this conclusion came from God, it is still treated as gospel.

What is to be inferred from the edict is that the apostles' commissions were revoked by God and in effect Christ's kingdom mandate was surrendered (and confined) to the church. Never mind that scripture clearly states apostles are to preach the kingdom of God and the gospel until the end of the world. More precisely, they are to preach it to bring the world to its Maker's predestined end. In their place, apostolic administration and the office's executive duties and responsibilities all passed to the bishops the apostles put over the works they founded. The prevailing

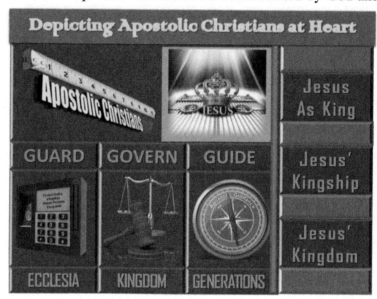

attitude was that congregations needed bishops at home to regulate them, to function as sort of "stay at home parents", since apostles were always away fulfilling the Great Commission.

Resented for being absent, perhaps due to not birthing enough apostolic leaders, apostles were supplanted for constantly being away capturing the nations for Jesus Christ's. They seem to have been caught in an ongoing tension between conquering new territories for Jesus Christ and comforting their converts, and between, discipling nations to His way of life or pastoring their churches. Besides all that, who could know how true the "stay at homers" conclusions were, since the capacity for widespread, in the moment communications did not yet exist. What they felt may well have been assumptions born out of frustration over the warfare and the ambitions of those in their ranks. Either way, confirming truth and having the benefit of up to date reports was difficult back then, leaving those out of touch with what their itinerant apostles were doing to arrive at the conclusion that rejected apostleship altogether. The situation harks back to Aaron's answer to the people that fumed over Moses' prolonged trip to the mountaintop to meet with their God. They felt that he had abandoned them and demanded are replacement.

Deprived of our modern technological advancements, forced pedestrian travel, and a dark energy-less world, those leading the church over time became convinced apostleship was obsolete. The growing Christian community concluded that apostles, as the early church knew them, were extinct more and their ministries no longer needed. Despite there being no way to know for sure that what was not happening away from the home front ceased to happen anywhere; the errant or hasty conclusion was ratified and permanently canonized as God's will. It was official; bishops replaced apostles over the church, period! Evidently, being absent or shut out of the process forever sealed shut the door that closed the apostles out of the works they birthed. A noteworthy feature of the dogma worth pointing out is that all discussions and deductions appear to focus mainly on revelation and teaching. The other ongoing aspects of the apostles' kingdom duties are not stressed in the "handing off, torch passing" language of the edict.

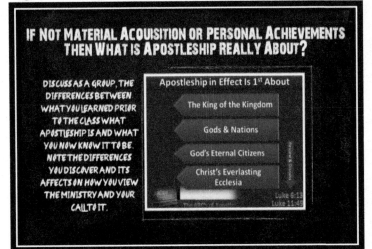

As you reflect on how something like this could happen, remember that back then there were no telephones, postal services, or any other media of immediate or timely communications to keep the apostles in touch with their works. What they did away from home base sometimes took years to get back to their congregations, that no doubt felt abandoned under the pressures of being a Christian. All communications were delivered on foot or by horses during that age. So while the logical delegation of the routine care of the church and administration of its affairs made sense to the apostles, their surrogate leaders took advantage of it.

However, nothing in scripture suggests or makes provisions for the bishop to replace the apostle over time. The act is especially questionable given the bishop is confined to the ecclesia while apostles originated basilically. That means, the office was instituted under God's theocratic realm, in an era where monarchies and not presidencies ruled. And since Jesus is a King and His realm a monarchy, establishing apostleship in such an age is well justified. Ordaining it to exist from age to age all the way into eternity serves God's purposes well, because the afterlife is monarchical, not constitutional. Insofar as the switch from apostolic to bishopric leadership over the Lord's church goes, the Catholics' biblical recount of the Dogmatic Constitution implies that controlling what the apostles did and treating them as authorities over the works they founded in their absence became increasingly difficult. Eventually it was seen as senseless. With long periods passing between their visits, it proved to be more expedient to reorganize the church's ministries and territories under bishops, than to have important details and decisions linger until the apostles returned from their missionary journeys. While it made perfect sense from a functional standpoint, it should be repeated that their decision might have been logical; it was just not scriptural. Such prudence should not have had in view the abolishment of the apostle's office altogether.

The only thing the council decreeing the new order saw that their congregations would lose by eliminating apostleship were the powerful demonstrations of the Holy Spirit - the miracles, signs, and wonders that define apostles. Otherwise, what apostles did (administratively and legislatively) the bishops, it was concluded, could do equally well. As for the apostles' potencies, it was decided that the church could pretty much get along without them. Closing down apostleship was taken as the will of the Lord, since no other office seemed to be endued with the dunamis to display its proprietary signs. Since scripture is the only place to locate the

APOSTLES MOVE YOU FROM:

- THE OLD TO THE NEW
- FROM GOD'S OUTER COURT TO HIS INNER COURT
- FLESH TO SPIRIT
- THE SPIRIT OF THIS WORLD TO HIS SPIRIT OF LIFE IN CHRIST
- DISCIPLESHIP TO SONSHIP
- EARTHBOUND TO HEAVEN DRIVEN

TRUE APOSTLES MAKE YOU COMPATIBLE WITH THE ENTIRE GODHEAD.

apostles of the Lord Jesus Christ, and His church for that matter, it is also the only place to look for what the Lord authorized humans to do in His stead. Regarding this provision, searching the Bible carefully shows you that it is not there, in spite of the edict being given the power of canon by human will. You might ask how humans could do such a thing. By what authority or right did

Short Answer to:
Apostle Bishop Controversy

a) Apostle pre-church
b) Bishop post-church
c) Apostle kingdom
d) Bishop ecclesial
e) Apostle global
f) Bishop congregational
g) Apostle appoints bishop

Apostleship encompass Bishopric reverse not the case.

they feel empowered to remove an entire office from the New Testament Church's ministerial ranks, not to mention, its founding office. The argument used is that since the letters penned by the apostles and circulated as God's ecclesial government were received and written by men, then men could overturn them at will. It is what they did back then and what thousands of church leaders have done since then, and are still doing today. Ask yourself why you stopped hearing the scriptures preached in your church or why you no longer learn about the Holy Spirit, the divine executor of Christ's New Testament will. The answer is humans usurped

Christ's authority over God's ecclesial spheres and responsibilities. They took over what He delegated to His Spirit to do for Him.

In contrast to church dogma, scripture presents an opposing view of the apostle bishop controversy. The famous in our times Ephesians 4:11 scripture emphatically contradicts it. If other parts of scripture are to be taken as perpetual then so too must the passages that seem inconvenient at times. In this particular instance, the inconvenience regards apostleship. Contrary to later church government, Paul in 1 Corinthians 12:28-29 flat out refutes that apostles are done away with, or that God ordained the office to be abolished. Instead, he asserts that the Lord's divine order over His church and kingdom is "first apostles". Later writings have never revoked that order, nor can it be proven that the Holy Spirit legislated its revocation. In fact, the reverse seems to be the case. The Lord keeps calling people to be apostles, ignoring completely various church councils' difficulty with them. If you are a Bible believing Christian, read the referred to passages yourself and you will arrive at the same opinion. Before you assume that this information is irrelevant to you consider this: Apostolic Christians are particular guardians of God's kingdom, which is why the ecclesia was birthed by apostles and not the other Ephesians 4:11 offices (or ministers if you prefer, which are officers of a government). Jesus summoned apostles to His commission and delegated it directly to them. Being an Apostolic Christian gives you the very responsibility for God's truth as He does His apostles. However inconvenient it may be to the established religions and their orders at times, you too must defend and flourish what God brings into existence on earth.

About Apostolic Christians

Proverbs 2:10, 11 says, "*When wisdom entereth into thine heart, and knowledge is pleasant unto thy soul; discretion shall preserve thee, understanding shall keep thee*". Wisdom, even under

developed wisdom exudes from Apostolic Christians. Particular markers identify apostolic believers that begins with how they see God and their duties to Him; a few more things that classify this kind of Christian as "apostolic". Apostolic Christians are biblical and scriptural, even if they have yet to learn the full word of God. Whatever portions of it they encounter ignites a voracious appetite for God's wisdom. The scriptures fill a great void for these people as long awaited answers to their issues are quickly spotted. This believer's constant responses to them include "so that is why...", or "that answers so many things for me." Thus, another key aspect of this convert type is ready reverence for God's truth, even His

enigmatic ones. You should know, however, that the two terms biblical and scriptural do not exactly mean the same.

Being biblical speaks to the Bible being the principal anchor of Apostolic Christianity. Being scriptural refers to these believers' utter reliance upon every word that proceeds from God's mouth. Both traits work to God's advantage since He wants Christians armed with the ability to spread His word convincingly that are committed to promoting His progress in the world. As if the above were not enough, here is another compelling thing about Apostolic Christians. They are loyal to the Almighty beyond just being His children saved by grace. Their

loyalties sympathize with the Savior's eons-long battle with other gods, and their deadly agendas against Him. A keen awareness of God's endless struggle with the rebellious powers of darkness leads Apostolic Christians to refuse to say there is no such thing as a devil. They will also not tell you that Satan or God's spiritual world are unreal, or equal to His.

For instance, very few Apostolic Christians believe in accidents, knowing that in reality there is

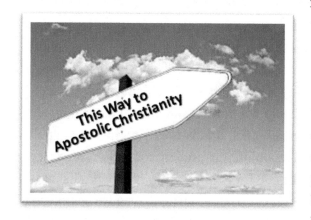

no such thing. "God is in charge of it all, period", is their credo. So this type of Spirit filled believer treats earth's oddities as unspectacular because they discern their behind the scenes sources orchestrating them. Affected but rarely shocked, they respond to spiritual phenomena by shrewdly dealing with its origins. Uncanny instincts apostolic disciples to detect when the Lord's glory or possessions come under attack, and when His boundaries are being breached. Their reaction to both can be aggressive. As converts to Jesus Christ go, those called to apostleship today are a special group endowed with exceptional perception and wit.

Redemption imparts to them peculiar capacities that must be nurtured by an apostle's wisdom to enable them to thrive apostolically and to explain intelligently apostleship's benefits in their lives. When such Christians are well equipped, they expound with confidence on the reasons why the Lord keeps sending His first officers into a world that resents and resists them. As a result, intelligence and boldness are two resources that God multiplies His Apostolic Christians. The boldness is not just to stay saved, nor is the intelligence simply to witness the gospel.

What the Lord gives this brand of saint detects threats, confronts and refutes error, and withstands fierce opposition. Apostolic Christians are kingdom minded even when they have yet to grasp what that means. They sense that there is more to God than His local churches but still see it as their duty to somehow protect and defend the Lord and His body. These converts keenly watch over what He brings into existence. You see, to these believers, salvation (indeed life itself) is more about the Lord than it is about the Christian's faith. However, taking our origins and foundations into consideration, apostolic convictions are why the Lord needs millions and millions of this type of Christian in the body of Christ today.

"TRULY, TRULY, I SAY TO YOU, WHOEVER RECEIVES THE ONE I SEND RECEIVES ME, AND WHOEVER RECEIVES ME RECEIVES THE ONE WHO SENT ME." -JOHN 13:20

In addition to Christians who can win souls, share their testimony, and settle into churches, the Lord needs Christians who really "connect" with His sovereignty as well as His salvation. He needs Christians that do not want to change Him or envision changing His world when they get there. The Christian convert God seeks refuses to downgrade Jesus Christ's works and will never blaspheme His holiness. No matter how popular it is to do so in modern times, Apostolic Christians do not disparage or violate God's righteousness to show how 'cool' He is. They understand the inspiration behind such tactics and are acutely aware that the Lord is looking for sons and daughters who hallow Him. Apostolic Christians know that God is utterly disinterested in mortals that seek to make Him fit in with other gods. The Almighty is not a pantheon deity, which is what bearing the title almighty means. These Christians know the Lord rejects any attempt to reform Him to make Him compatible with fallen humanity. God is holy and He likes His holiness. The conflict arises when darkened human minds try to interpret and apply His superlative holiness. Holiness to God is more than restraint, it is prudence and discretion. It is practicality guided by wisdom, caution, and thoughtfulness. It is purity without prudishness. Despite people's issues with His holiness, God considers it His best self in and given He has existed forever; He sees no reason to change or downgrade Himself. Holiness means more to the Lord than any of the creatures He made could ever know. Christians appointed to apostleship share His eternal citizens view of their Maker. They revere God as creator of all because that is what makes Him unique.

Our Lord stands in a class of His own. All of these examples are why Apostolic Christians are greatly trusted by God. He trusts them because He knows they will remain on His side. God is confident these Christians will steadfastly uphold His Son's kingship and guard His kingdom, because spiritual guardianship, church safety, and kingdom security are at the heart of Apostolic Christianity. Besides all of this, is this type of Christian's heart and soul integrity. Blessed with a resolute righteousness compass; when Apostolic Christians vow to the Lord, they mean what they say. As true replicas of His character, they press to pay their vows even when it hurts; and diligently watch over their own words to perform them, as they know their God does.

Attributes such as these are why the Lord is discipling Apostolic Christians. He values them because they love His truth and prize His wisdom. Years of trial and error confirms that He can trust them to represent Him properly. Such believers hunger for the Lord's mind; they do not dread having to learn Him. For these people, engaging in authentic Bible studies and taking Christian classes is exciting. When the true and living God is preached or taught, it is never boring to them. Instead, they find themselves invigorated every time they encounter their Lord, coming alive at the sound of His word. Above all, they do not as Proverbs 27:4 says *"envy the wicked"*, which is why they are not normally tempted by modern culture and its trends. Irritating to the world, the Apostolic Christian is a *kingship* thinker. This believer truly lives for God's way of life. He or she easily discerns the ridiculousness of the seductions that aim to invade and pervert God's children, and do not buy into any of it. These are courageous people with minds that are often very difficult to change. And by the way, accusing them of narrow-mindedness will not deter them; many of them see it as affirmation and not embarrassment.

All you have read so far should explain vividly Apostolic Christian's almost insatiable appetite for God and His word. The explanations given tell you what makes them accept His truth as the answers to life's perplexing issues. They see it as fresh and relevant no matter how long ago scriptures were written. You can add to what you have read how much these saints value being God's children. Each one sincerely wants the world to meet their Dad and its God. As dear sons and daughters, they desire others to come to know the gracious living their Heavenly Father prepared for those who love Him. As His faithful offspring, they yearn for their Father's heart's desire, which is for the rest of their brothers and sisters join the family. Empowered with potent spiritual fervor and compelling charismata, they without tricks, hyper-emotionalism, or manipulation take up their charge and do their part in the family business; a part they know reaches all the way into eternity.

Make no mistake about it, these Christians are extremely passionate about their Lord and are determined to promote His glory. Reverential restraint balances their motivations; they want to see the Lord win back what is His <u>every</u> time. So they avoid discrediting Him with coercive acts that put people off, or devious tactics that mislead those coming to Him into thinking that He is more indulgent to sin and worldliness than He is. Both are seen as sleight of hand tricks that attract numbers but fail to produce genuine converts. Christians of this sort loathe putting God at a disadvantage or shaming Him. When or if they do, it grieves them bitterly. By no means seen as perfect in their own eyes, these souls are constantly driven by the Lord's ceaseless perfecting of their beings. It is why, those to be expected human trip ups and missteps (given our *treasure is within earthen vessels*) are quickly acknowledged and rejected. In this respect, Apostolic Christians follow King David's model. They swiftly repent of realized sin, and address its causes promptly. Rapid resolution of their human frailties makes these children of God brave, even when they do not want to be, because of utter agreement with the Lord's way of life. One thing they do not subscribe to is "tempting the Lord their God". These believers do not frustrate God's grace, but are realistic about their own humanness.

Destiny Apostolic Christianity

**Kingdom of God
Home of Apostolic Christians**

Repeated and habitual sin is scorned by this type of believer. As Christians go, they are as sold out in secret as they are in public and will fight hard for God's righteousness, often harder than they fight for their own rights and privileges in Him. Apostolic Christians believe that God too has rights. They harbor no misbeliefs about His sovereignty, His love, His holiness, or His compassion. They furthermore do not exploit His mercy and grace. The words of 1 Peter 3:12, 13[1] rules how they partake of His benefits. These saints do not seek to abuse God's goodness or assets, but instead look to manifest His fullness in their lives and others. Somehow, these people come to know the Lord in ways many saints do not and perhaps cannot, and that makes them peculiar. Here is a passage of scripture that paints a fairly good picture of the Apostolic Christian today. It comes from Malachi 3:16-18.

> *"Then they that feared the LORD spake often one to another: and the LORD hearkened, and heard it, and a book of remembrance was written before him for them that feared the LORD, and that thought upon his name. And they shall be mine, saith the LORD of hosts, in that day when I make up my jewels; and I will spare them, as a man spareth his own son that serveth him. Then shall ye return, and discern between the righteous and the wicked, between him that serveth God and him that serveth him not."*

[1] Cross-reference Peter's words with Isaiah 8:13. Sanctify means to set apart, consecrate, hallow. God is not to be lumped in with your perspectives on other deities or their faith but is to be viewed as unique and treated as exclusive and superior to them. This He expects you to do from the inside out. The Lord demands to be enshrined in your heart, your emotions, beliefs, passions, and desires. He does not expect to be blended with the other spiritual or religious options available to you.

Look at how affectionately the Lord expresses His appreciation for this group in the passages. Their allegiance to Him in the face of the atrocities and abuses He suffers move God to write their names in a special registry that He calls "The Book of Remembrance". It is so uncommon for the people of earth to remain faithful enough to Him to resist the world's cultures and compromises that the Lord determines to claim these believers as His own special treasure. Their loyalty deeply encourages Him in His struggle with the hostility and treachery of their day. So God vows to remember to reward their devotion after He settles the score with those that hate Him. This tender side of God and His gratitude are often lost in the overwhelming criticisms that Satan's propaganda machines spew out against Him. Discerning believers know the truth behind the hateful things unbelievers say about the true and living God. The ability to resist the temptation and not buy into it and sell God out is great. That ability is why those that fight temptation are noted in God's "Book of Remembrance". Deception is really why it is only in scripture that true believers find the answers to the irresistible love they have for the Lord and their fervent desire to remain faithful to Him. It alone explains the unshakeable faith that grips their hearts. These people, though unable to say why, just cannot turn their backs on God. As you read on you will see why this is the case for you who are appointed by Him to become Apostolic Christians.

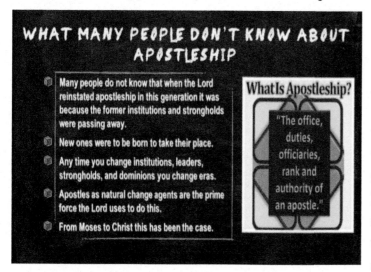

Amassing Apostolic Christians and engaging in astute but practical apostleship discussions promises the apostles of today will no longer have to struggle to be taken seriously. That alone will go a long way to their being welcomed in the established ranks of mainstream Christian ministry. Eventually, the incredible stigma attached to their works that causes them to suffer chronic setbacks will be erased as a result. After all, modern apostles' hardship is largely due to having too few disciples to build and sustain their commissions. Thus, the primary barrier to their success and growth is acceptance that relies on understanding, theirs and others. People must understand apostles to appreciate them. However, the apostles must likewise understand the people of their day and make themselves and their offices clear and believable to them.

Acceptance of any kind relies on believability. So, the more apostles get Christians after their own kind to believe in their right, better yet their duty to exist, the more their works will flourish like the other fivefolders' do. Large numbers of faithfuls advocating their ministries will see to it. These achievements will end apostleship's bitter clash with traditional church dogma and inspire those ordained to Apostolic Christianity to accept it and serve boldly, and enthusiastically. Ideally, over time, the entire 1 Corinthians 12:28 and Ephesians 4:11 team will bond and the Lord will be better served by it. That is when His end time harvest ministries actually perform His will.

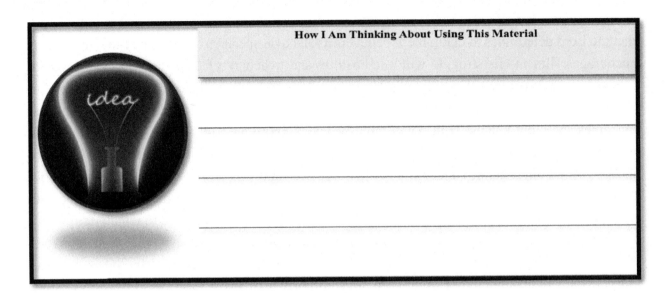

How I Am Thinking About Using This Material

UNIT 2
The Foundation

This teaching as you have seen so far makes a powerful case for discipling Apostolic Christians. It shows you, who are Christ's seed, the importance of exploring your next role in God's kingdom as a Christian. This guide shows you how to give careful thought to your next step and why it must include deciding if an apostle is the best minister to get you there. The wisdom of such decision-making has to do with guarding your salvation in Jesus Christ. With our Lord's faith coming under ruthless attack every day and from everywhere, the pressure to defend Him and His redemption as our eternal heritage is greater than ever. Apostleship is one of the recurring instruments the Lord uses to confront turbulent periods in His church's history.

What I Want to Go Over Later
1) Biblical Christianity
2) Persuasive Answers
3) Returning to the Bible
4) Converting From Christ
5) Scriptural Salvation

If you as a Christian are wondering what is the best option for your growth and advancement in Jesus Christ, you should know that not all ministers are constructed or endued by God the same way. What highly developed apostles are designed to help you do in God is quite different from what the other ministers can produce in (or impart to) you. For instance, not too many apostles realize that there is a proprietary[2] power and stewardship attached to this office. Acts 2:42-45; 3:32-35; 5:12, 13 all declare it. As a matter of fact, power is supposed to attend every apostle's ministry, despite the number of those today declaring it does not have to. Power, unusual exploits, are innate to apostleship and only those who are really bishops or church appointed instead of Christ commissioned apostles lack it. With their patented resources and through the exercise of the office's exclusive power, apostles settle and secure the Lord's church. Scripture and church history tell us that apostles are especially built and outfitted to get the church through seasons of heinous assaults, and to resettle it when its foundations are shaken and must be restored. That alone may give you strong reasons to become an Apostolic Christian, considering the state of the church today and the world's ire with it. To clarify this for you as a case in point, take the Lord's parables of the stronger man that can plunder an uncontested (or vulnerable) strongman's house and palace in scripture. See Matthew 12:29; Mark 3:37; Luke 11:21. The parables recount how Jesus subtly introduces Himself as heaven's strongman, sent to earth to cast out the wicked spiritual strongholds that control the world's powers.

As the Almighty's sent one, the Messiah appeared on earth to cast out the god of this world. The parables recalled provide a good example of the weighty mantle the Lord puts upon His apostles. He heavily endues them because apostles are the Lord's chief defenders and the kingdom's equivalent of spiritual (or principalic) strongholds. They are that is, if they understand His issues with earth and the human experience. Those that do not eagerly sidestep their call to address those issues for Him and flounder in their apostleship, bringing no fruit to maturity. But apostles are not the only ones God depends on to defend His faith and protect His interests. The everyday saint is expected to do so as well. The apostolic ones are inherently most driven to do so.

Truthfully, many devoted believers today would defend their faith if they could. They just do not know enough about what belonging to Christ really means fight for it. A large part of the body of Christ is just flat out underdeveloped. As God's people of today, they to falter in their faith and constantly grope for persuasive answers to their convictions. As a result, the modern Christian is frequently at a loss to explain biblically Christ or His beliefs. Of the many reasons

---

[2] Branded, exclusive, patented, private, protective, territorial, watchful: On that possesses, owns or hold exclusive right to something as its proprietor. Merriam-Webster.

for this, the major one is because the very scriptures that saved their souls have essentially been erased from countless church sermons. The help that they should get from God's word is denied them in favor of strengthening the worldly bonds enslaving their souls. This tragedy among other things make defending our Savior impossible, which is of course he point. Few vessels of God's Spirit are equipped enough to take on the daily barrages that challenge our faith. Most of Jesus' converts cannot answer basic questions about their salvation, not to mention Christianity in general. Deprived of the spiritual nourishment that comes only from feasting on God's word of truth, they are too malnourished to confront, let alone endure the persecution that comes with belonging to Jesus Christ.

Modern Christianity is presently more embattled than any other religion. Its sheer size and global dispersion make it so. There are significant numbers of Christians in every nation on earth. The body of Christ, on account of this, must learn to neutralize the belligerent machine agitating Christianity to wipe it from the world's recognized and respected faiths. God's people are the only ones legitimately qualified to stand against it. They alone, because they are His offspring and embody His Spirit, have the wherewithal to push back on it. Christians' descendant's status obliges them to preserve their Savior's work and to see that He is not diminished or dethroned from His lofty place in the  world. Today, savage assaults on Christ and His church work deviously around the clock to dismantle the very truths that define our uniqueness; to whittle the Lord's ecclesia down in order to overthrow it eventually. Intimidation tactics use cruelty to terrify the Lord's people out of enduring to the end. You however, do not have to yield to it, and this book shows you how to overcome it all. Its insights map out for you the ways you can steadfastly resist God's enemies while it can still make a difference. Once you learn who you are in and to Christ, you can come through the assaults with your faith intact, and maybe even stronger than before. However, the first thing you must accept is that it is the Lord and not just His church under attack. In fact, the attacks take aim at Him through His church. Apostolic Christians most of all can appreciate this although many of them just need to learn, and how. Still, the right perspective leads to the right answer and course of action. Knowing where and how it all began helps a great deal.

The first attack against the Lord was on His church. The initial target was the authenticity of His word, the Christian's Holy Bible. Devious mind games maneuvered to scrub scriptures' power from the doctrines it teaches to discredit it in the world. The effect of the attack has been numerous congregations ceasing to teach the Bible as God inspired and intended it to be taught. It resulted in thousands of modern churches choosing to promote the teachings that convert Christians to this world's culture rather than to protect our Founder's faith, and His two thousand plus years of ecclesial success. These are other reasons why the average Christian is unable to distinguish those who are Christ's from the children of darkness. Do you remember Malachi 3:16-18? The end of that referred to passage says, *"Then shall ye return, and discern between the righteous and the wicked, between him that serveth God and him that serveth him not"*. Revisit the 18th verse. Here is a more modern way of saying it: *"Then you will return and distinguish between the righteous and the wicked, between one who serves God and one who does not serve Him"*[3]. As it stands now, we believers can hardly tell who is who in the body of Christ and what is and is not God. But as we multiply Apostolic Christianity, we will be able to do so again with great certainty.

Culture crafted (and at times demonically manipulated) preachers teach Christ in a way that neutralizes His truth and tricks His people into embracing the world, thinking they are enjoying His salvation liberty. The Gates of Hell that Jesus condemned has revved up an evil political machine to persecute the church bitterly, and to sabotage the effects of His Great Commission. A commission that Jesus commanded His ecclesia to fulfill throughout the church age until He returns. A commission that, by the way, was first given to and initiated by His apostles. Stifling the church's outreach denies Christ His end time harvest, the objective of it all. Today's fiery barrage is catching Christians up in the world's ruthless discrimination strategy to snuff out the church's light and life in the world. Antichrist laws and judgments that destabilized the Lord's ecclesia turned Christianity in on itself, making it fear spreading the gospel and converting souls to Christ. The present church turmoil is the most pressing reason why God is dispatching apostles. It is also why they in turn must disciple Apostolic Christians, ministers, and members to their commissions; the type of Christian whose witness and actions go beyond evangelical soul winning to kingdom keeping.

Apostolically primed converts to Jesus Christ see guarding the King of the kingdom as the sole means of guarding His ecclesia on earth. They know that a kingdom without a king is unprotected and vulnerable to a takeover. It is quite like what is happening to the kingdom of Christ on earth today. God's adversaries know that separating Jesus Christ, the King, from His kingdom's citizens casts Him out of the human heart temples He occupies. The effect is His enemies take over His earthly conquests. To retake His control from the fallen angels that made themselves into gods, Christ must return His wayward believers to the one true God. When He does, He gets a modern version of the believers that took the world from polytheism to

---

[3] Tree of Life Version of the Bible.

monotheism. To make it so, today's apostolic leaders must disciple and empower converts to help them.

To oppose the cross, unprecedented hostility against Jesus Christ and His church strikes at the very lifeblood of our beliefs; which is why so many Christians though alarmed by it feel powerless to do anything to stop it. To identify the ancient roots of our persecution and its real objectives, read Psalm 2. It talks about how the kings of the earth galvanize against the Lord and His Christ. That scripture is why Jesus decreed the Gates of Hell would rise up against His church but would not prevail. These realities are why this training was written and why you need teachings like this one to stand, and to stand therefore. **Question**: What is an apostle? For the answer, see the tab below for a quick answer to what an apostle is.

What Is An Apostle?   "A sovereign's sent one."

Why You Need This Information

The main answer to why you need this teaching has to do with God birthing and making apostleship (apostolic) Christians, now and in the future. It is a brand of believers in Christ Jesus raised up to counterbalance the evangelical Christianity that dominated the world front for so long that by all appearances seems to have surrendered God's people to it. Apostolic Christian is a term that in the not too distant future, you will hear everywhere. Why? The answer is because Apostolic Christianity is the only thing that can come from the Lord's wide scale reinstatement of apostleship at the head of His church.

After all, nothing less can be expected from an apostle's ministry than populating the Lord's kingdom and church with the same type of Christian that defined His early believers. Completely absorbing their converts into His being characterized the first apostles' works. Multiplying Jesus Christ in earthly form motivated their worldwide spread of His gospel and their efforts did not just focus on adding members to their congregations. They focused on multiplying the Spirit of Jesus Christ <u>first</u> and planting churches to house His converts <u>second</u>. What these statements declare then is that all who are saved by Jesus Christ are undeniably Apostolic Christians, whether or not they profess or know it.

Gather in a circle to Think up innovative ideas on how this wisdom should be spread throughout the Lord's church today.

The church being birthed by apostles from its inception makes it apostolic at its core. It is King of kings redeemed, kingdom born and bred, and kingship nurtured. Evangelicalism does not define the New Creation church of the Lord Jesus Christ, despite it taking God's glorified Son to the world; however, apostleship does. Sovereignty, not just soul winning, keeps the church. The latter may populate it, but the former secures it. Evangelism (soul winning) is only a small, albeit significant part of the church's Great Commission. The most involved and endless part

of that commission is "teaching". Once souls are born again they must be taught. Not just about their salvation, but also about their citizenship in the kingdom of God and Christ. Jesus started His ministry preaching the kingdom of God and of heaven, not salvation. If you review the scriptures, John the Baptist preached being saved and then later the Apostle Peter did also on the church's first Pentecost. Between these times, the Lord Jesus brought His kingdom to earth, preached it and commanded His apostles to do the same. Presenting the King of our kingdom is most important since it identifies the convert's destination, which is leaving the world for Jesus Christ a Sovereign Savior.

The Lord Himself mentions being saved around twelve times and salvation maybe twice. More than a hundred times, as the Messiah, He speaks about His kingdom in the gospels. These approximates do not diminish the need for salvation or its preaching, but they do imply that He put more weight on living His eternal kingdom life because a baby is only born once. After entering the world, the entirety of the infant's existence shifts to its lifetime. The same is true with the born again child of God. Once the penitent is born from above, there is nothing left for its birthers to do except hand it over to its nurturers and rearers. Everything that happens after the natural babe exits the womb concentrates on growing and thriving in life on earth. The same is true with the spiritual babe; all focus shifts to adapting newcomers to God's eternal kingdom to His way of life, which involves discipleship, spiritual growth, ecclesial education, Christian maturity, and kingdom profitability. Guiding the Lord's converts throughout their earth walk predetermines a saint's eternal place and reward in heaven, and when heaven comes to earth, thereafter.

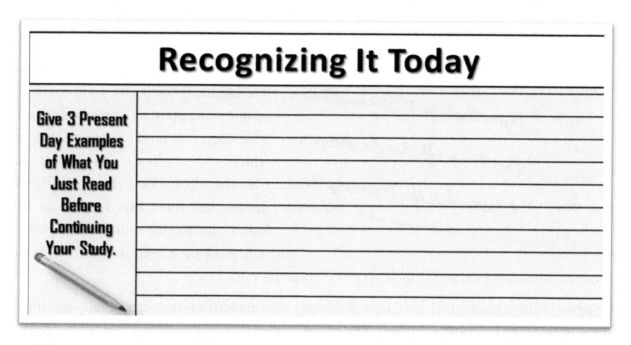

The Kingdom of God, the Kingdom of Heaven

More than 125 times the Lord Jesus refers to the kingdom of God or the kingdom of heaven. One must wonder, in view of that number, why He thinks it is so important. Could it be because as a Sovereign was sent to recover His citizenry? Is salvation the entry into His inheritance and not the total inheritance itself? It would appear so from the scriptures. The apostles discerned the Messiah's emphasis and likewise stressed the kingdom of God and Christ. This conclusion has to do with how the Bible portrays Christ, apostleship, and His church. It shows that apostles converted the first Christians, founded the New Creation church, and shepherded Christ's first century converts until enough ecclesial ministers were born again and conformed to His way of life. When capable servants could take on these duties, the apostles delegated them, freeing themselves fully to the word of God, prayer, and fasting. As the believers multiplied in number and increased in Jesus' kingdom knowledge and competencies, the apostles put their routine duties into the hands of the developing ministers, who were rising in their ranks. In this way, the church's other ministries were born. That foundation is concentric to the Christian church's divine legacy. It further explains why 1 Corinthians 12:28 starts with "first apostles".

What I Want to Go Over Later

1) *Protecting our Lifeblood*

2) *Apostleship Converts*

3) *Apostleship 3 Strengths*

4) *Fending off the darkness*

5) *Eternal Life Principles*

As apostleship becomes more defined, and over time established, its converts will increase and become more apparent. That is just what the Lord wants. To succeed in His endeavor though, the Almighty needs bona fide, well-trained apostles and apostolic ministers to send into His field. After all, one can hardly claim the Lord is raising up and using apostles en masse and miss what they will produce when He does, which is millions of apostolic[4] Christians that reflect His first officers' mantle, and mentality. Ideally, as His highly developed ministers, apostles will produce a well-discipled body of apostolic ministers to expedite their apostles' commissions.

Begetting believers after their own kind is the only way modern apostles can be fully reinstated at the head of the Lord Jesus' church. The sole way to do that is by staffing their commissions with compatible, apostolic disciples and laborers. Accomplishing this calls for clarifying apostles' worth to God's kingdom and Christ's ecclesia. Doing so will permit the pulpit and the pew to grasp and cooperate with God's Apostleship Reinstatement Campaign. For revelatory purposes, you should know that a *campaign* is a movement, a crusade, and or an operation. It is a promotional drive, a military fight, and a combat battle. Campaigns are clashes between opposing forces that are competing for the same conquests.

Campaigns, Apostles, and Warfare

The campaign war connection enters apostleship when you add the words struggle, camp array and campgrounds, and battle to the list of definitions, because they too are included in the word campaign. These terms explain why Strong's concordance calls apostleship a warrior's

---

[4] For the purposes of immediate identification with the apostleship in general, the word that is more familiar 'apostolic' is used more than the New Era Apostleship™ term for the type of Christian to come from 21st century apostles' work. It is the more accurate term for what we are producing for Christ is "apostleship Christian" rather than "Apostolic Christian". The reason for the distinction is to separate the Bible's brand of Christian from that of the "Jesus Only" faith, which is not what New Era Apostleship™ Restitutions aims to promote.

campaign where military service engages one in an expedition that pits soldiers against opposing forces. Discharging apostolic duties, Strong's likens to warfare, which is why Paul calls a part of a commission a spiritual warfare. *Strateuomai*, Strong's G4754, ties warfare to apostleship. The term equates apostleship to a military career as a soldier in active service, what Paul tells Timothy. But here is the clincher; executing the apostolate comes with arduous duties and functions that contend with deeply rooted in carnal inclinations. It is a reality that goes to the core of the office's definitions. They specify the ministry treatments apostle deliver to those they serve and lead.

By now, you sense that much goes into informing your people on Apostolic Christianity enough to motivate their desire to be transformed into one. That work begins at the top. From the head down, you must make this revived brand real, attainable, and enjoyable to them. In keeping with the top down conversion model, you should prepare your closest leaders to take a major role in your Apostleship Discipling Project.

Begin by training your first string leadership personally. Be sure to include in that training how to transform your people. All members should participate, even your youth department. Leave no group out; make your ministry interactions one hundred percent apostleship. This approach takes the anxiety out of the transition and makes everyone feel comfortable about it and their part in it. Make the shift valuable to <u>all</u> concerned! Now is the time to start thinking about how you and your leaders will take and maintain control over the events of your transition to apostleship.

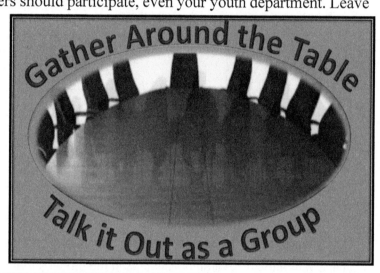

This information merits further discussion, so gather in a group and explore its implications to come up what some of the nuances of apostleship that many people heretofore have overlooked.

Work It Out: Plan a Campaign

What is God's campaign you ask? It is New Era Apostleship™ Restitution, and initiative to install apostles at the head of His church. It is launched to bring it back into His divine order according to 1 Corinthians 12:28 that declares, "first apostles". Complete the following activity before you resume your reading.

With the goal of this training being discipleship, use your history and experience with this mainstay of church development to imagine the best way to disciple those in your sphere to Apostolic Christianity. Outline with a team the first to last steps in the process that you would say are the most ideal for this objective. Use the comprehension and question guide below to guide your discussions, planning, and strategy. Conclude with a project that focuses on how you will accomplish your goal, when and where you will launch it, and the best team of people to help you get it done. Make sure you outline some of the talents your team will need to succeed in your approach. Conclude with how you will register those you recruit to Apostolic Christianity, and what you plan to do with those that you convert to settle them in this Christian emphasis.

What's the Next Step?

How Do I Create the Apostolic Christian Buzz?

Where is God in His Reinstatement Campaign Now?

Where God's Apostleship Reinstatement Campaign stands today is with many modern apostolic leaders and their people being largely unaware of apostleship as an arming, as well as an equipping and empowering office. God sees the mantle as undeniably martial, which is why He designed it to function that way. If this is not the case, why else refer to the apostles, generals? Remember the word *strateuomai*. What apostleship does best is win people to the Lord Jesus Christ from the fallen gods their parents served and passed on to their offspring.

Here is the main reason apostleship is about gods and nations. Another thing apostleship is good at is motivating converts to trust and submit to God's sovereignty and not just drift through life on earth on His salvation. Never forget that for true apostles, it is always about the King of kings and His global dominion. Apostles help Christ's family appreciate the difference between God's sovereign righteousness and His kingdom citizens' rights, a distinction that often eludes many of His leaders. Another thing that apostles do best is arm God's people to fend off Satan's darkness, as Jesus reveals to Paul in Acts 26:18. In studying current events, most of you will probably agree that apostles' absence is sorely felt in view of today's church's fracture and instability. Their suppressions completely changed the status of the once widely Christianized world.

Besides the martial dynamics of the office, apostleship also has a strong revelatory component. Christ passes on His own mantle's revelatory doctrines to His apostles in a way that secures

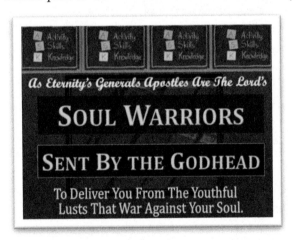

His converts. Those revelations answer their salvation questions with patented apostolic wisdom that prepares them to master His eternal life in principle and in practice. Additionally, apostleship distinguishes itself by also disarming Jesus' enemies. They do this by dislodging their holds on the people who come to Him. Once they are liberated, apostles' freed converts publicize God's love and culture throughout their generations. If that sounds simple to you, rest assured that it is not. When you try to walk it out in the everyday world, you will find it not to be easy for the apostles or their followers. In spite of its difficulties though, Christ's apostles succeed at it because their unique ministry edge is strengthened by the powerful revelations they receive from God.

Group Reinforcement: Gather with your study group to discuss and relate apostleship's power to dislodge God's enemies from the souls of His people using the scripture below.

Put It to Work Exercise

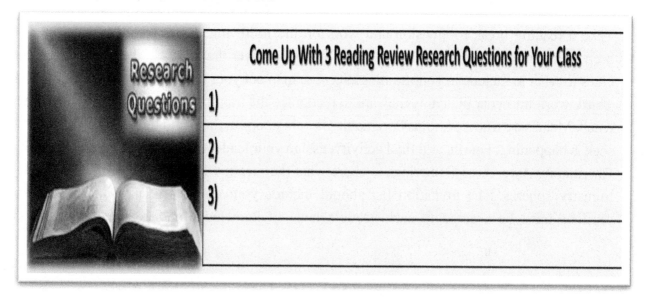

Working It Out <u>Biblically</u>

Activity Breather

Take a reading break to envision and work on the following. First, consider how you will prepare and introduce the training to your leaders. Go over the words in the mosiac for some clues to what to include in your training. Second, map out your leadership conversion process. Third, work into your plan how they are to recognize the training and its success in those they teach. Make sure true Apostolic Christianity is being born in them and that the conversion you seek is happening. Fourth, as a final activity, assign your leaders to plan and sponsor Apostolic Christianity Awareness Gatherings to share what they learn with those in their Christian and ministry spheres. The invitation list should include your entire organization, even if the sessions must be adapted to each group's level of knowledge and conversion readiness.

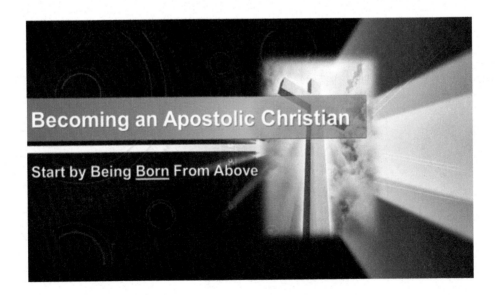

UNIT 3

Learning Apostles as Revelators

Throughout the New Testament, apostles are pictured as revelators sent from God to broadcast His word on earth. The reason is they are commissioned to make Him and His kingdom known to our world. What the Lord sends apostles to broadcast are His world's realities and truths, two things they know are not always the same. The Lord specially outfits them to make His story make sense in this life. New Creation apostles of Jesus Christ release electrifying revelations that uncase the mysteries of God's kingdom[5] and its eternal communities. Refer to Hebrews 12:22-24 for the source of this revelation.

Uniquely endowed with exceptional revelatory insight, the Lord's apostles are indoctrinated with what they are to dispense from His heavenly libraries. Largely legislative and constitutional writings penned long before and since the foundation of this world, baptizes apostles into God's celestial domains. Total immersion is how they learn what transpired before earth and humanity were created. In private sessions with the Risen Lord, apostles are instructed on the portion of the Creator's archives that articulates their earthly service as ambassadors of the King of kings.

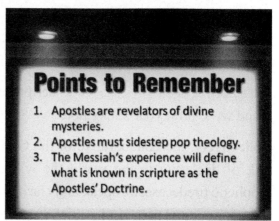

Points to Remember

1. Apostles are revelators of divine mysteries.
2. Apostles must sidestep pop theology.
3. The Messiah's experience will define what is known in scripture as the Apostles' Doctrine.

---

[5] 1 Corinthians 4:1.

The All Important Apostleship Prophecy Connection

In closed Messianic meetings, apostles are presented with the eternal plans and purposes the Lord devised when there was just Himself and the rest of the Godhead. Being the proactive Maker that He is, the Almighty wrote out how life on earth would go for Him, His Son, and their creation, when as yet none of it existed. What He wrote to govern and guide His creation, the Highest God kept secluded in His archives until time came to prophesy it to this world. Voiced as His hidden plans, prophecy allows the everlasting God's secrets to stream His eternal mysteries into our world.

Bit by bit, and messenger by messenger, the plan kept secret from the foundation of the world unfolded until scripture's Author made His way into the planet. According to all that was written of Him, Jesus the Sovereign of creation who pronounced the prophecies concerning Himself to the Old Testament messengers, donned flesh and became Savior. Once the prophecies that predicted, confirmed, and crucified Him were fulfilled, He returned home to pass the torch to His Holy Spirit and through Him, His apostles. The torch-passing conclusion comes from Acts 1:2-4. Notice as you read it that during His forty-day post resurrection crash course, Jesus stays with what launched His earthly ministry in the beginning, the kingdom of God. As you meditate on the scripture, try to imagine what is peculiarly insightful about it and write it on your sticky note.

What Is Peculiar About Acts 1:2-4?

1-
2-
3-
4.
5.
7.

Collectively, the collaborative of the Godhead, its apostles, and later the church took up the task of declaring to the world the will and work of God and Christ. Apostles, like their prophetic predecessors, speak and clarify the eternal mysteries the Creator concealed in Christ for preappointed times in His history. Look at Isaiah 48:16 for God's powerful declaration of this through one of His major prophets.

Genuine apostles take God's mysterious truths as their official seal. They publicize heavenly secrets the world has yet to receive that are essential to its advancement, and its end. And, they use His Old Testament scriptures and His Holy Spirit who inspired them to do so. This indispensable apostleship trait is often detected by those who encounter the office and its mantleship, even if it is not so readily understood at the time. What is not always so apparent is the subject and substance of apostles' mysteries.

Before getting into that, take a moment to do the following Active Reading Exercise and then read on to learn about the 21st century apostle.

ACTIVE READING EXERCISE

Relate a Scripture	Connect Your Related Scripture

Write Another Question	Answer Your Question

Suggest a Teaching Idea	Describe Your Teaching Idea

Twenty-first Century Apostles and Heaven's Mysteries

Interacting with 21st century apostles may not always surface the often vague or enigmatic nature and content of heaven's mysteries they carry. This means that the deep seated mysteries' and their character are not readily discerned by those unfamiliar with apostles or apostleship. Consequently, the nuances in their teachings can easily be overlooked or dismissed as vague. As an Apostolic Christian, you should accept that <u>all</u> of God Almighty's apostleship mysteries and revelations are *exclusively* about Jesus Christ, the Son of

God. Frequently, His tightly secured truths get lost in pop doctrine or historical church reformation theology. Sometimes that is intentional by God, and at other times, it is a consequence of spiritual blindness. Both are remedied by His apostles.

Devoted apostles are neither as easily distracted from God's eternal truths, nor quickly captivated by supposed new revelations. With years of the Messiah's royal doctrines embedded in the apostles' psyche and sculpting their intelligences enable apostles to see through His imitators' tactics. That is what makes them acutely susceptible to the Lord's Spirit and the organics of God's word and chief authenticators of its truth. It makes what they glean from God to be organically authentic apostleship truths. Authentic apostolic doctrine strictly focuses on Jesus' life: eternal, past, present, and future. His apostles are consumed with their Sender and publishing His experiences with His heavenly and earthly creations as disclosed in scripture. These are what comprise the dutiful apostle's mysteries. Any so-called gaps people find in scripture, are filled by the Holy Spirit who ceaselessly streams God's original texts to His apostles. That is how revelation knowledge is always made readily available to those that rely on Him. At this point, you should be admonished not to confuse the unknown or enigmatic with revelation. They are not the same, and you could be duped into believing error simply because you never heard information before. Revelation is more than facts or tidbits of history. It is part of God's ongoing disclosures that He has been unveiling since the foundation of the world hidden in Christ for the church.

The mysteries that God hid in Christ to conceal His secrets from the world come alive to His apostles. With near perfect clarity they declare what is customarily hidden in God's secret library. His highly classified revelations preoccupy the dedicated apostle who is caught up in the Messiah's passions, hopes, and dreams. Tapping into His ageless annals, future ambassadorial messengers retrieve the revelations that scripture identifies as Apostles' Doctrine. Their communications bring the King of kings' thesaurus of heavenly mysteries to earth. Truly converted apostles of Jesus Christ are the ones entrusted with stewarding and dispensing eternal truth for Him. Apostles more than reveal God's truth, they also embed His existence in the soul of their cultures.

In the diagram below, write what you envision to be the determined Christians R.O.A.D. to becoming an Apostolic Christian.

Apostolic Christian R.O.A.D.
- ➢ **Revelation**
- ➢ **Of**
- ➢ **Apostleship**
- ➢ **Doctrines**

Notes

_____

_____

_____

_____

Apostles' Doctrines Communicate and Commemorate Jesus Christ

Apostles bring the world the Messiah's memoirs. Through their messages, they represent His eternal sovereignty and powerfully showcase His pre-incarnate career as Yahweh. Avid apostles unlock Christ's archetypal chronicles to decode scripture's disclosures of Jesus' pre-earth existence as creation's Sovereign. Driven by the fiery passion of a fully persuaded servant, they glorify and inwardly embrace the humility that drove a Sovereign to become a crucified Savior. Immersed in the disclosures of God's experience with His creation, apostles fuse with the love and commitment that drove Him

What I Want to Go Over Later
1) God's Eternal Mysteries
2) Isaiah 48:16
3) God's 21st Century Secrets
4) Apostolic Mysteries
5) Apostles' Doctrines

to suffer heinous atrocities at the hands of the creatures He made. Gradually, as the Lord replays His history for them, Christ's apostles more and more appreciate the reasons He sacrificed His own soul to be made sin for lost and dying humanity.

To assure they respond to His revelations responsibly, the Lord sees that His apostles know fully what made Him sacrifice Himself on the cross. He stresses that His disclosures are meant to inspire a conviction and persuasiveness that can only come from in-depth exposure to what made Him do it, love. Potent Messianic indoctrination takes scripture's accounts of Christ's life from an event narrative to a moving portrayal of a heavenly reenactment. Apostle's intimacy with the Almighty breeds in them the familiarity of an eyewitness' testimony. As a result of their powerful encounter with Jesus Christ, apostles tell His story not as if it is handed down, but as if the apostle literally witnessed it firsthand. Such communiques cohesively formulate the biblical Apostles' Doctrine, packaged as the Gospel of Jesus Christ.

Applying It Today

Give 3 Present Day Revelations that You Would Classify as Strictly Apostolic. Share Them With Your Study Group.	

The Gospels Demystified

What the Bible calls the gospels, apostolic messengers will tell you are incomplete synopses of what Jesus lived. They narrate how Jesus thinks and what He wants, and they predict the ways He has predetermined to have His way. Apostles know John the Revelator's word to be true. The then world could never contain the book's recording of the whole minute-by-minute story of Jesus the Messiah's three-year ministry. There is no quick way to cover the entirety God

Key Scriptures:
Acts 26:18
1 Corinthians 12:28
Ephesians 2:20

incarnate. Sabotage and loss notwithstanding, the Lord's church is therefore left with synopses, summaries, and brief narrations of what He did on earth. With that we are still awed and mystified by His life's works, with many at a loss to grasp fully the extent of His human divine work. That work the Holy Spirit will gradually unfold until the end of this age. By the way, here is something else you should know as an Apostolic Christian, Jesus did not bring a foreign mythic message to earth. He taught the writings of prophets that make up the majority of the Old Testament. Jesus brought God's past into humanity's present. Amazing their works are what the Holy Spirit uses to propel the Godhead past and present forward into humanity's future. What this means is that the whole New Testament unveils what the Old Testament prophesied about Yahweh's world, His soul, and His will. These are revealed as His character and inclinations. Scripture is more than a dogma or condemnation; it is God's heart and soul. It captures His

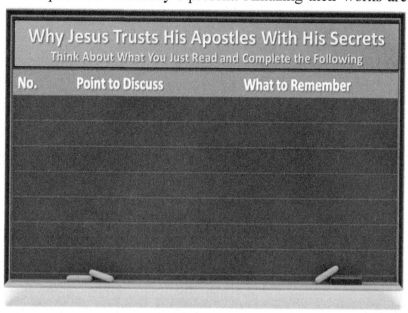

divine life experiences, and spreads it all to the world. To reinforce this requirement of their commissions, Christ bears His soul to His apostles to make His most secret self, known to them. The level of intimacy He establishes between them is to assure they are proficient in disclosing Him and His world to their world. These are the ways the apostles of Jesus Christ are confirmed as trusted stewards of His mysteries.

In-Office Intelligence

For the sake of the office and its objectives, the Almighty furnishes His apostles with insights and intelligences to popularize the Son of God and His lifestyle. It is to this end that faithful apostles emphasize the Lord Jesus Christ as the source, cause, and outcome of their ministry. On the other hand, those disloyal to Him will scarcely mention His name or bear witness to His life and purposes. Some go so far as to discredit or disparage Him, and forsake Him altogether. Others' messages are so murky on who He is and what He does that they come across convoluted. Any attempts such apostolic ministers make to validate themselves often lacks the affirming signs that normally accompany God's revealed truths. This seems to be especially so by His apparent silence today. God withholds His confirmations for the authentic, regardless of how much some of His servants try to mimic them through artificial means. Would you like some modern day mimicry (or gimmickry) examples? Here are a few that you might recognize.

One example of false or carnal validation is the contemporary minister's boast over the years about preaching the "kingdom", while ignoring its King. Another is how often you hear preachers say they are winning the world to Christ without ever mentioning His name, for fear of running off their converts. An additional case in point is the hundreds of songs from His supposed worship ministers (labeled Christian) that never name Him, just in case a secular agent wants to use their music for the world. Here is another one: the countless sermons that brag about discipling souls to Christ without preaching His gospel, or referencing His word at all. The tragedy of these misconceptions is that most ministers today do not know that to promote a state and conceal its leader is risky at best, and in Christ's day, it was condemned as treasonous. Before Christianity was a worldwide conglomerate of local churches, it was a nation-state begotten by Jesus Christ; and it still is. That nation-state is what will be transported to God's world as the ecclesia, not a scattered mass of individual congregations. This predestiny says why before apostles were set in the church, they were commissioned by a King to be His ambassadors to the world.

Ambassador Allegiance

In ancient times, and perhaps still today, ambassadors and envoys that diplomatized as a monarch's representative without ever naming their sovereign as their sender were indicted by their governments as traitors. Their doing so was seen as taking credit for the sender's accomplishments or attempting to usurp the sovereign in the eyes of others. Thus, an ambassador going in his or her own name, claiming to be sent by the head of state or an organization, was rejected as an impostor. In extreme cases, those attempting such were severely punished and even killed. Under threat of fatal consequences sometimes, ambassadors took strict care not to misrepresent themselves in order to avoid giving the impression that they came or spoke in their own names. To avert the perils attached to presuming to speak as a sent one, they declared at the outset whom they represented and what they were sent to do on his or her behalf. These fundamental elements of ambassadorship are deeply engraved in the template of all diplomatic agencies and functions. Meanwhile, in contrast to today's reckless trend, ethical[6] apostles for Jesus Christ were concerned with Him as the Lord. They wanted their Sovereign publicized. So for them, "it being all about Jesus", was not merely a slogan. It was their core, even if many of them needed guidance on how to express and promote Him loyally. Following is a table with three relevant statements on it. The first is "Salvation to Sovereignty", which means the Apostolic Christian sees and reaches beyond the sinner's prayer. The second is "First Apostles: Why" to reiterate that from Jesus' appearances onward, the Lord turns to His apostles to settle and resettle what He wants instated or restored. The last

---

[6] Unfortunately, ethics with the Lord Jesus Christ is often dismissed, if it is ever considered at all.

statement is "Apostolic Christians make the Best Commission Team." Although not too much had been said about the commission team, enough has been mentioned to let you know that apostles cannot just appoint or rely on any Christian to see to their commissions' success. They must choose and use those that are most compatible with the mantle and its office.

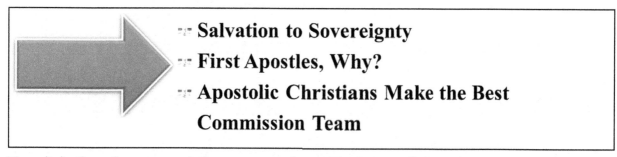

- Salvation to Sovereignty
- First Apostles, Why?
- Apostolic Christians Make the Best Commission Team

Now it is time for more reinforcement actions. Shed some light on what you just learned. Review the lessons it gives Apostolic Christian as a group, and then in the end put all the pieces together.

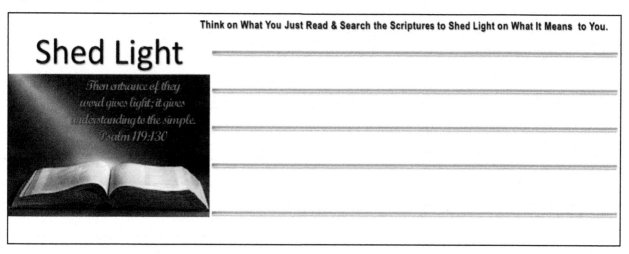

Think on What You Just Read & Search the Scriptures to Shed Light on What It Means to You.

Shed Light

Then entrance of they word gives light; it gives understanding to the simple. Psalm 119:130

Making More Scripture Connections

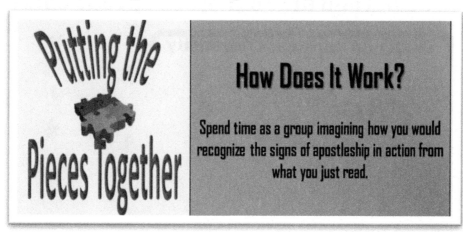

How Does It Work?

Spend time as a group imagining how you would recognize the signs of apostleship in action from what you just read.

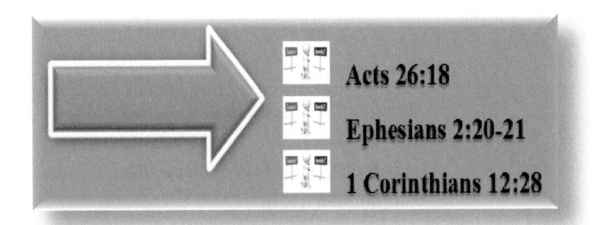

Acts 26:18

Ephesians 2:20-21

1 Corinthians 12:28

Making Strong Bible Connections

1. _____
2. _____
3. _____
4. _____
5. _____
6. _____
7. _____

Go Beyond the Four Walls of Your Church

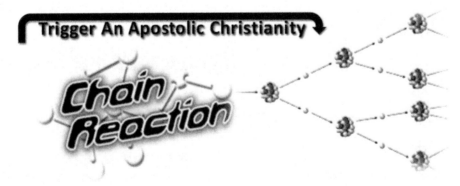

Trigger An Apostolic Christianity

UNIT 4
Jesus, Jesus, Jesus!

If you ever meet and spend time with a real apostle what you will hear almost nonstop is "Jesus, Jesus, Jesus". Of late, that kind of fidelity is becoming increasingly uncommon. It is regularly mocked and reviled. Deep affection and complete devotion to the Lord are presently considered to be outmoded because worldliness scorns the passion that surrenders a minister to Him. The type of preoccupation with the Lord that validated the early apostles is routinely lacking in many donning the title of minister of the gospel today, let alone in those donning the title of apostle. In contrast, biblical apostleship refuses to succumb to the pressure that inspires modern disloyalty to God. His inner restraints on their souls bind fidelitous[7] apostles to His will, and to the archetypal parameters He preset for the office.

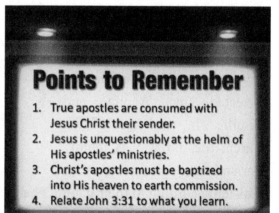

Points to Remember

1. True apostles are consumed with Jesus Christ their sender.
2. Jesus is unquestionably at the helm of His apostles' ministries.
3. Christ's apostles must be baptized into His heaven to earth commission.
4. Relate John 3:31 to what you learn.

Aside from innate convictions of who (and what) Jesus is and being persuaded of the infiniteness of His power, apostles are regulated by potent internal constraints. Indescribable controls prevent the real ones from straying from the Lord. Here is another way to tell the false from the true. As a result, these apostles see their principal responsibility is to represent the throne of God and to serve the preeminent sovereignty of the Lord Jesus

---

[7] Fidelitous: Having high fidelity.

Christ. Wholly consumed apostles promote the King first and then His kingdom, not the other way around, as is frequently the case in the modern church.

To explain further, Christ's converted apostles feel that since they are called by Jesus (authorized and sent by Him), logically all they do should revolve around Him. An attitude that is no different from the person who is committed to his or her company. Conversations about their employer from devoted employees would mainly revolve around the company they greatly esteem. It is no different with apostles in God's service. Based on this, you can see why if Christ is not at the heart of an apostle's talk, He is not the force driving the apostle's work. If He is not at the center of the apostle's endeavors, it is because He is not at the helm of the apostle's ministry with one possible exception. That is in the case of the immature apostle who is to be distinguished from the false one, despite their manifesting the same way at times.

Immature and False Apostles

Apostles who are not fully baptized into the King's apostleship commission can far too often launch their ministries, or eventually shift their messages to represent and promote this world. (A concern voiced in John 3:3.) This happens to untrained apostles because they begin as gifts and omit becoming officer trained. Without that training, novice apostles stay in the ministry gift mode and never quite extend their initial calling and its resources to a particular commission.

Devoid of little more to talk about than what they grew up on, new apostles can appear to be false when they are simply unlearnt. Many of them can only preach the old as the new, the way Apollos did before he was corrected by Aquila and Priscilla. In this age of the church, the old way is mainly charismatic. Unlearnt apostles

Christ's Apostles
1. Let Him drive their work.
2. Keep Him at the helm of their work.
3. Keep Him at the center of their endeavors.

minister according to their natural charisma and not so much according to the grace that God exclusively reserves for His apostles. Here is how the Apollos account goes:

Apollos was a great orator in his day and as such assumed he could just <u>add</u> Jesus' gospel to his customary mosaic message. Although he was ordained to become an apostle eventually, it was not until he connected with the Apostle Paul and learned from him that he transitioned from an apostolic gifting to enter the apostle's office. Starting out as a young orator in the beginning, encountering his mentor transformed Apollos' *ministry* calling into an apostleship commission. That shift began with his encounter with Aquila and Priscilla. Apollo's state of mind and ministry attitude before then was somewhat the way it was with Moses who received God's call to rescue His people. With a different expression, but same motivation, both men raced ahead of God in answering their callings propelled by what they had always done. In Moses' case, enthusiasm caused him not to wait for God to reveal the entire Exodus campaign to him. He acted on impulse and tried to defend God's people in the flesh. Similarly, Apollos "jumped on the bandwagon" when he realized the old was passing away and Jesus's new order had arrived. Fascinated by the move, he rushed in with what he had instead of learning the fine points of what God was replacing. Both men's lack of knowledge left them to fall back on tradition to answer God's summon to the new, thus putting new wine in their old wineskins.

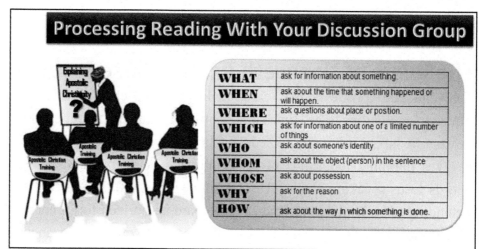

These examples show how complete conversion to anything new is improbable without the training that distinguishes the similarities from the differences of what was and is from what is to be.

Until they are properly developed, untrained, and unconverted, apostles speak as gifted orators and articulate historians. They typically declare the old in new contexts. Eager to get on with what they feel they are summoned by God to do, they dodge readiness to get "out there", so to speak. In their haste and naiveté, these novices are convinced they are promoting the new thing God is doing, when in reality they are just overlaying their old ways with a new veneer. A similar thing happened to Stephen the Martyr. Failing to discern what separated the Apostles' Doctrine from his historical knowledge of Yahweh and Judaism, and his religious experience, Stephen launched out on his own to do what he thought they were doing. Unfortunately, his recklessness ended with fatal results.

It is time now to work out some of your thoughts on what you learned. After completing the next exercise, read on to detect what else separates true apostles from the false ones, and why you as an emerging Apostolic Christian should know how to do so to safeguard your earthly future and your eternal destiny.

Write a Curiosity Question	Answer Your Curiosity Question

The Jesus of Nazareth vs. the False Jesus Apostle

The bona fide apostle knows that God has age-old enemies and Jesus Christ has ruthless impostors pretending to be Him. They know that Satan has not given up on recouping his losses and that he labors ruthlessly to seduce Christians back into their old lives. His favorite tactic involves dumping thousands of false ministers and antichrists on a generation. Scripture records Jesus speaking about false and antichrists more than once. He said they would come pretending to be Him before, and as if they are authorized forerunners of His second coming. He gave specific signs in Matthew 24 and Mark 13 to guide those sincerely awaiting His return to keep them from being deceived. To become a trusted apostolic minister is to accept that Christ's adversaries become yours in the way His advocates become yours as well. The point of this discussion is this.

As a rule, apostles constantly preaching and propagating world cultures cannot be sent by the true Jesus, Jesus of Nazareth. New or untrained apostles, as it has been explained, are the only exceptions to this rule. However, if they like Apollos submit to quality training and education, they can become vessels worthy of the Master's use. When such apostles do submit to training, they will eventually swap their novice impulses for the message and mantle of the Lord Jesus Christ and His early apostles. Whenever that takes place, young apostles become revelators of God's mysteries and stewards of His otherwise unfathomable truths. They cease to be propagators of world culture and devilish doctrines. Give some thought to how you will share this teaching with a young training resistant apostle you know or may meet. Use the space below to jot down some ideas and then continue your reading.

Write a Teaching Idea	Explain Your Teaching Idea

Take a moment to consider the passage and the statement. Afterward, do the SCRIPTURE R.E.M.I.N.D.E.R. EXERCISE to list some of its insights in the space below. Discuss your responses with your study partners. Afterward, read how to go on to perfection.

SCRIPTURE R.E.M.I.N.D.E.R. EXERCISE
"Let this mind be in you, which was also in Christ Jesus…" Philippians 2:5

Scripture Study: **Revelation** - **Explanation** - **Mysteries** - **Insight** - **Need** - **Demonstration** - **Example** - **Relevance**

Put some thought into the scripture passage below and respond to it according to the R.E.M.I.N.D.E.R. Exercise. Give your scriptural impression of each of the following based on what you just read.

R.E.M.I.N.D.E.R. SCRIPTURE: 1 Peter 2:19

Revelation

Explanation

Mysteries

Insight

Need

Demonstration

Example

Relevance

Going on to Perfection

On the surface, underdeveloped Apostles' Doctrine starts out carnal and saturated with worldliness. That is why they appear false, except to the discerner who recognizes them as immature. Unfortunately, it is also why their disciples remain unchanged and immature as well for all the time and money they invest in the young apostle. Their messages may be fiery but seasoned saints know they have a long way to go to become transformative. Pop doctrine, slick slogans, and trendy theology are what you get from them, because it is all they have to offer until they grow and learn the fullness of God's truth and wisdom. At the outset, their words differ little from those of the false apostle, as they cannot yet consistently discern untruth from distorted truth.

When you first encounter the youthful zealot, their exuberance is so infectious or impressive that you overlook their skimpy knowledge and incompetence. You excuse their mistakes, writing them off as immaturity. It takes a while for you to move from desiring their charisma to demanding their competence. At this point, you urge the newcomer to get the education that guarantees both. If the novice is conscientious, he or she will take the advice and enroll in a good program to train the natural charismatic capabilities for God's service. If not, you will be dismissed as a long line of critics they have brushed off.

Don't Second Guess Yourself

Some novice apostles seem mature because of the messages they pick up from older ministers. The maturity you hear comes from the words used, not from the messenger. To explain, mature words copied from another can make a speaker sound mature. If they stay on script, you will believe they are, but when they go off script, what is in them is all that can come out. It is then you realize that they never internalized the message they preach, they just memorized it. Training is the only way for the words they hear to penetrate their ignorance and breed the wisdom that transforms both theirs and their hearers' souls. If they learn and stay faithful to God, a fervent pursuit of His kingdom righteousness and truth takes over. Completing the training will ultimately transform the beginner into the masterful servant the Lord deserves. The same holds true for the training resistant apostle, differing from the novice only in the refusal of knowledge. Giving up the training resistant stance on apostleship ministry would improve them as well.

You will know the training resistant apostle by their boasting concerning years of service and their pride in not having to submit to learning. In essence, the training resistant apostle's substance and delivery sounds a great deal like the novice's words. Both messengers' words are skimpy and only sporadically accurate. The absence of education can make the novice's error sound much like the counterfeit apostle's falsehood. One is the victim of misinformation and the other has chosen deliberate deception. Without looking deeply, it can be hard to distinguish them; still both put the Lord's kingdom and its citizens at risk. The determination to skip quality education and training leaves a discernment vacuum that education alone fills. The vacuum, called a knowledge deficit, occurs because the filters that guard and enable the novice and the untrained to detect evil, and recognize the paths of God's righteousness are missing.

The major sign of an apostle's humility and maturity is awareness of the high premium God places on aptness in His[8] ministers. From Genesis to Revelation, aptness in all respects surfaces as His gold standard[9]. The Lord requires those who will serve and represent Him to learn Him and to learn of Him in order to discern how He ministers. Scripture demands and affirms education and training's preeminence by showing how God uses and gets more from the learned than He does from the unlearned. From Enoch, Noah, Abraham and Moses, all the way up to the first apostles and the early church, the exhortation to become knowledgeable and expert in the things of God is a constant. In considering this, think of the Apostle Paul, the latecomer to Jesus' college of apostles. Although Paul never walked with the Lord or studied under Him directly, he nonetheless is credited with writing a good part of the New Testament's epistles. Why is that? The answer is because of his prior education, which only needed to be sanctified and amplified by Jesus Christ to articulate the eternal things the Lord left with His apostles before He returned home. Without quality education and instruction to back experience and practice, many ministers will never reach beyond the novice realms in their service to the Lord, no matter how long they serve Him.

Apostleship Starts With a Message...

THE TRUE TEST OF APOSTLESHIP IS HOW THAT MESSAGE:

1. Attracts a following
2. Matures followers
3. Founds an embassy
4. Converts to the kingdom
5. Motivates Support
6. Builds for the kingdom
7. Embodies the King
8. Guards and exalts Jesus' kingship
9. Promotes God's Sovereignty
10. Enlarges, enriches, and empowers the kingdom

A ministry novice, no matter how sincere of heart, will feel the effects and detriments of the Lord confining all on earth under the darkness of sin, and realize that sin includes ignorance. God withholds wisdom until there is a kernel of it in the heart to appreciate His word and bear Him good fruit. The reason the Most High God hides His knowledge for those

---

[8] For the sake of clarity, the word means, appropriate, suitable, fit, proper, proper, capable, competent, able, skilled, clever, quick, ready. These synonyms equate to the following descriptions of "gold standard", the person, or thing that is the most satisfactory, appropriate, pleasant, and effective, of the highest quality, etc.

[9] For application purposes, a metaphor for the best or highest, the gold standard of something is simply a great or excellent example. A gold standard is the best of the best and also a test or measure of comparison that is considered ultimate or ideal. In the above context, gold is used to mean symbolically, a system, benchmark, yardstick, touchstone, criterion, and paradigm. A standard of value that is considered to be the best used to judge the quality or level of other, similar things; a paragon of excellence. The supreme example of best, most reliable, or most prestigious thing of its type against which others are judged or measured, the best available thing of its kind.

that He trusts is obvious, and inspiring to the knowledge hungry. The competence-driven expect to have to dig and climb and sometimes claw to get God's best. On the other hand, those who cherish their gifts and talents above the intelligence of God's Logos—logic—will find the Lord's standards tedious and unnecessary, since all they want to offer is the exercise of their gifts. Training is a time waster to this ministry group, because they are too eager to display their talents to concern themselves with standards or competence.

Impatient ministers are hasty whereas avid learners are cautious; aware of the danger unlearned and incapable servants pose to the Lord's kingdom, church, and ministries. That risk alone should serve as motivation enough to forsake ignorance and fully embrace knowledge. Conscientious versus charismatic driven apostolic ministers will submit to training and readiness to protect and keep what the Lord entrusts to them in a condition He can use. Those that pay the price will find the Lord replacing early-misguided zeal with His wisdom and truth.

ACTIVE READING EXERCISE

Suggest a Teaching Idea	Describe Your Teaching Idea

Germane Apostleship

The word germane refers to what is relevant or usefully connected; what is suitable for a particular purpose or comprehension. The word's basic meanings soundly wind down this subject. Here are some sobering thoughts for you to ponder as you prepare for your next exercise. The following gives you concrete reasons to embrace and value apostles. When you are under apostleship that stays with what the Savior deposited in the world and inseminated in His church, it will separate you from this world and its cultures. This outcome is what is meant by "Germane Apostleship", and what the Messiah is speaking about in John 17:17.

When praying to His Father in heaven, Jesus asked Him to "sanctify them by thy truth; thy word is truth". Organic[10] apostleship, mentioned earlier, separates you from sin. It never makes you comfortable with reminiscing or returning to your pre-Christ life. Nor does it venerate godless freedoms above the liberties provided in Jesus Christ. Organic

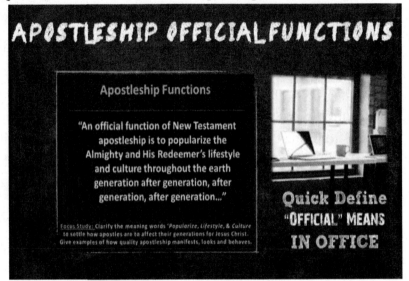

apostleship teaching comes from God's throne and Christ's mouth. It reflects their heart on humanity and its righteousness or sin, as well as their mindset on its solutions and condemnations in the world and after death. As with any good agent or representative, faithful apostles do not rewrite God's rules or vilify His holiness.

The Nostalgia Ploy

The ploy to get you to abandon Jesus Christ and renounce your salvation is a serious one. The powers of darkness that lost you to Jesus are mad and vicious about recovering you for themselves. To get a picture of how their most common ploy looks, here's an example. Take as a case in point, the countless converts to the Lord Jesus that relish retelling their horrid "before Jesus saved them" testimonies. The way some saints retell it, you almost think they regret that He did. In addition, they seize every opportunity to recall their unsavory pasts that you can almost recount them by heart as they recall them. When you look at them recollecting "how they used to be" you can almost see glee come over some of their faces when they remember how *evil* or *bad* they were or how their former wicked deeds bought them respect with the unsaved, "before they were saved." Let me say at this point that this example is not

---

[10] Living, completely; natural, unrefined, unprocessed, pure, raw, and nonchemical. Once seen as instrumental for all that it touches or that is to come from it. That which is grown without the use of artificial things, fundamental, and systematic. Whatever constitutes the law by which something governed or organized exists: Adapted from Merriam Webster online.

referring to the Lord using a redeemed person's pre-salvation testimony as a healthy or soul delivering tool. I am talking about how some people can only go back to their before Christ days to praise God. With these people, Satan often employs distasteful reminisces as a temptation device to tarnish their redemption. He does so because nostalgia is a powerful ally and so a reliable ruse against God's saints.

The Devil likes the nostalgia ploy because it uses the memory and dissatisfied emotions, or carnal cravings to revive old passions. Recalling fonder times (always inaccurately) spawn wistful desires in unstable converts that seduces them to cherish past sin as fond memories. Inspiring these people to relive forgiven sins often enough short circuits the soul purging that cleanses their consciences from once habitual dead works. The objective is to con the discontent into seeking some good in what the Lord delivered them from, so that they never quite accept how abhorrent their former beliefs and appetites really were in God's eyes. The ploy's advantage is that it reserves what appears to be future backsliders or compromisers for the Devil that will cast deciding votes for his way down the line. The "times were easier before Christ" scheme is how the church began the downward spiral that led to its present decline.

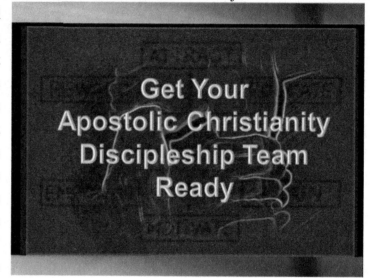

To spot the nostalgia ploy in action, pay attention to how "old life testifiers'" tone changes when they talk about how different their life in Christ is today. Sometimes they almost sound as if they are yearning for the excitement of their former lives. The problem with it is that as believers grow, their testimonies should contain more of their triumphs in Christ, than celebrations of what they gave up for Him. Maturing in the Lord ought not to be eclipsed by His children's nostalgia over their old ways. Constantly reliving their old life could mean the Messiah's salvation only superficially affected them, implying that the convert has come to regret His redemption of their soul.

While this explanation definitely does not characterize all Christian testimony, it surfaces in far too many believers in Christ's church today. The compulsion to rehearse pre-Christ sin repeatedly as one's only testimony of God suggests the testifier has forgotten the sorrow that came with their ungodliness, and the gratitude they felt when the Lord first took them out of it. This one example shows you how people can become dangerously comfortable with reminiscing their past sins and fall prey to the Devil's "return to the wild" call unaware and backslide or sell out Jesus Christ without meaning to.

What has the above to do with apostleship you ask? The answer is appreciation. To benefit from the apostles, the Lord assigns you to, you need to appreciate the mantle's potent keeping

powers.[11] As Messiah's heaven sent warriors, apostles are motivated by a determination to shore up, and to sustain your growing faith. Through both, they solidify your conversion to Jesus Christ, that is, if they themselves have been fully converted[12]. Those who are fully converted deliver messages and counsel particularly composed to keep you in Him, and to safeguard you from the invisible forces that resent

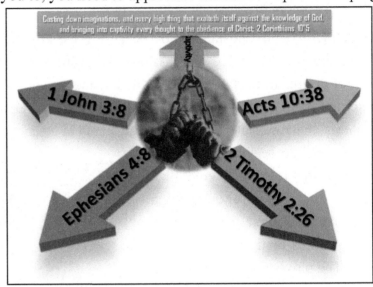

your redemption. Highly trained apostles have tangled with the deadly captors the Lord set you free from more than once, and learned how determined they are to regain your soul. No genuine apostle is deluded about the brutal hostile forces that trapped you in the past. All of them know God's adversaries will do anything to resume control of your life; and see it as their duty to alert, preserve, and shield you from them, if you let them do so.

Moreover, God's wisdom and history have taught seasoned apostles that the best way for demoniacs to recover you for Satan is through nostalgia[13]. It works because the memory can be a stockpile of nostalgia when it is packed with disappointment, discontentment, and spiritual unrest[14]. When converts fail to renew their mind by the renewed spiritual mind they receive from Christ, their memories make ready tools of deception or apostasy later. These along with boredom are all used to woo you back to your soul's old captors. Apostles' are ready for your old soul captors' game. They know they will never stop trying to get you back. Triggering deep longings for your old self[15] is how they get you to give up on Jesus Christ and come back to them. But you should know that often you return to them in spirit and heart long before you manifest your departure from the Lord outwardly. Veteran ministers know the signs, as do

---

[11] Acts 2:42.
[12] 2 Peter 2:19.
[13] Jeremiah 7:24.
[14] 1 Peter 5:8.
[15] Ecclesiastes 7:10.

veteran saints. They know you are only fooling yourself. To keep up the charade, you may still go to church, but cannot wait for it to end. You may still tithe, but resent having to give your money. You may still pray but find it increasingly harder get into it, and dread reading your Bible because of its conviction. You may attend worship services but wonder why that is all you can do, yearning inside to check out the old haunts. Lastly, you may still love your Christian friends, but find them dull and seek out some of the people you "hung with" before you were saved. When these darker emotions and thoughts are challenged, you become belligerent and defensive. Although you have already turned in your heart, you are unwilling to acknowledge it. But the spirit that recaptured you for Satan is already celebrating the win.

Once you abandon Christ, you become a spiritual orphan, which is how your soul's old captors step in to reinstall their former strongholds in your life. When they are in, they pressure you to backslide and exchange the true Christ for a false one; and here is the tricky part: much of this happens beneath your subconscious. On the surface, they lull you into thinking you are in control; deep in your soul, it is another story. A sinister machine works underneath your intelligence to transfer your will[16] from the Spirit of Christ back to theirs[17]. The Devil's scheme works best when Christ's adversaries can convince you that you are still with the Lord. Spiritual blindness may prolong their success, but by the same token, it also assures it. So they can wait for however long it takes your will to reward their success. Once they have sold you on nostalgia, reentry is imminent. In addition, your former enslavers have no problem with you appearing to live in both worlds, serving both deities at the same time, as long as what you do exalts them, not your Maker.

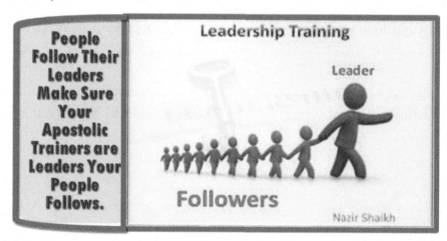

---

[16] Romans 6:16.
[17] 1 Timothy 3:7; 2 Timothy 2:26.

M.I.N.D. the Word Activity

"For who hath known the mind of the Lord, that he may instruct him? But we have the mind of Christ." 2 Corinthians 2:16

The M.I.N.D. the Word Activity seeks to guide your personal use of the scriptures in your daily life. It gives you the opportunity to fuse the passage's wisdom with your soul and then allow it to instruct you on the behaviors that you feel you need corrected, to properly fulfill your duty to God's truth in action. Study the following scripture's potential to do this for you. Be guided by what you have learned so far.

Scripture: John 17:17

Motive: <u>Why did God include it in His Bible?</u>

Answer:

Instruction: <u>What does God want to teach you from this passage?</u>

Lesson:

Necessity: <u>What about your beliefs or behaviors make this passage necessary for you?</u>

Issue:

Duty: <u>What must you do to observe, conform to, and practice this word every day?</u>

Change:

Now paint a practice picture of your R.E.M.I.N.D.E.R.S. and M.I.N.D. Your Word Activities

Reading Review

1. Apostles are God's revelators.
2. Apostles unlock God's mysteries.
3. Apostles bring the world into the Messiah's memoires.
4. Apostles are all about Jesus, Jesus, Jesus!
5. Underdeveloped apostles can appear false.

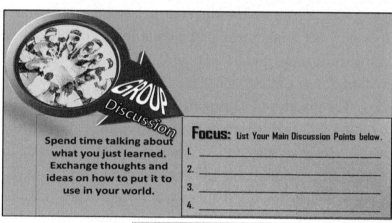

GROUP Discussion

Spend time talking about what you just learned. Exchange thoughts and ideas on how to put it to use in your world.

Focus: List Your Main Discussion Points below.

1. _____
2. _____
3. _____
4. _____

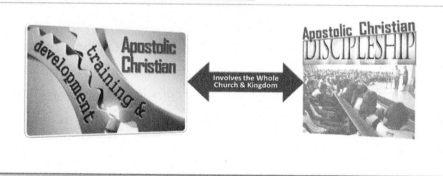

Apostolic Christian training & development

Involves the Whole Church & Kingdom

Apostolic Christian DISCIPLESHIP

Jesus' Kingship and Kingdom

Many Christians cannot appreciate apostles because they do not know why and how the Lord uses them. A significant degree of the arguments against them has to do with their worth to the body of Christ and their value to its faith walk on earth. Due to their absence from mainstream Christian ministry, believers question apostles' usefulness to their spiritual life and growth. Being devoid of their impartations for ages, many believers cannot fathom why they need apostles and most actually fear them. What God's family does not realize is that the breadth of hallowedness needed to live in God's world, and the power to thrive in His kingdom here, came to apostles first. These are two of the main reasons Jesus told them to "Be endued with power from on high". Transformed apostles are innately furnished by God with the answers to "eternal life", and the dunamis to impart eternity's virtues and strengths in their followers.

When it comes to how prized apostles are to God and Christ, the Savior anticipates perpetual reservations held about them for us in scripture. The best way to explain and relate to apostleship is in terms of His kingship, His eternal kingdom, and the nationhood that emerged from both once Jesus reproduced Himself. The first thing you must do to become and excel as an Apostolic Christian is to place Jesus' kingship above His kingdom, because that is the order in which they exist in His world. You may not think this important, but reflect on how often you hear the kingdom preached in comparison to the number of times His kingship is neglected in the process. Consider how many things you can say about the kingdom as you inwardly wish you knew more about your King. The practice of separating Christ and His church, His kingdom and His kingship, are the reason you find it hard to appreciate apostles or to place them profitably in your Christian walk today. Kingship and kingdom are where you begin to discover apostles' relevance, and not just in the church that has rejected them for so long. To grasp the magnitude of apostleship, you will have to trace it all the way back to Christ's world when He ruled the earth as Yahweh, and even before that. Without conception of His sovereignty[18] and monarchy, apostleship can be confusing, especially in view of contemporary church doctrine. It takes knowing the Lord as King first before you can understand His reasons for commissioning apostles. That is how Jesus presents Himself to Israel in scripture and how we, His church, are about to learn Him. The apostles realized it and never forgot it.

In the space below, write what this says to you and how it affects your attitude toward apostleship.

---

[18] Authority, rule, supremacy of power or rank, comes from sovereign that means superior, ruler, master, highest, supreme, chief, golden. Onlineetymologydictionary.com.

What I Now Understand and Can Relate to Others About What I Just Read

How God Summons and Appoints Apostles

Apostles are the equivalent of secular ambassadors who are sent out by the sovereigns of their lands. It is why Jesus as the Sovereign of sovereigns personally sends out His apostles. Based on most nations' diplomatic protocols, it is only the sovereign of the land that commissions an ambassador. With ambassadors being apostles' ecclesial counterpart, the kingship and kingdom of the Lord Jesus Christ is integral to how God summons and appoints these representatives of His throne. The reason He does so is that Jesus has been a Sovereign longer than He has been a Savior, a truth much of His body on earth either does not know or fails to appreciate. This fact, His apostles on the other hand, easily latch onto, penetrating its implications very quickly. Intuitively, they recognize that subtle tactics are always at work to downplay the Messiah's monarchy. Often without saying how, they shrewdly move to counteract or eliminate them. Apostles know that Satan's vow recorded in Isaiah 14 has not been revoked, only reassigned; he is as bent on overthrowing God's dominion as he ever was. So apostles are protective of God's glory in this world as a result. How do these statements affect your perspectives on apostleship? Say so below.

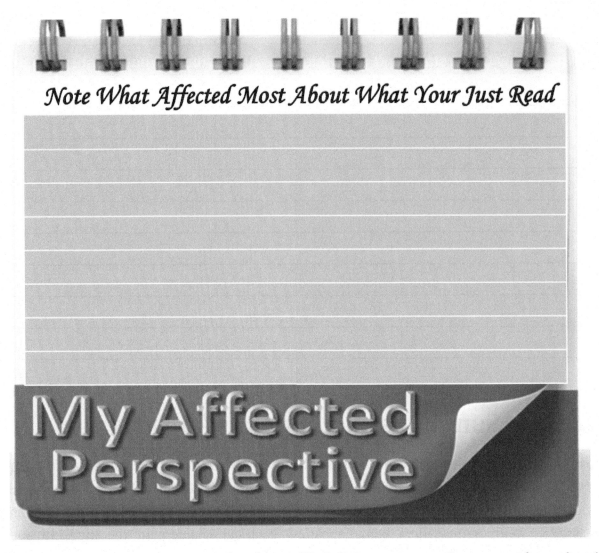

Note What Affected Most About What Your Just Read

My Affected Perspective

Apostles are keen among many other things. Their keenness comes from never forgetting that creation's Sovereign sent them, and what it is He commissioned them to do for Him. From these two convictions emerges a mindfulness of the importance of discerning their servanthood role in the Lord's life. Astute apostles resolve the double role they must fill to serve the duality of their Sender's existence. They are motivated by the fact that long before the Son of God came to save the world, He ruled it as its Creator. His pre incarnate state and its supremacy are why scripture calls His body "a nation of kings and priests", and why He declares we will "reign with Him on the earth". (Refer to 1 Peter 2:9; Revelation 1:6 and 5:10.)

As a Group Review What You Learned and List 5 Lessons Apostolic Christian Can Learn From It
1)
2)
3)
5)
What Statement Will Spread Apostolical Christianity the Fastest?

By now, from what you have read and what you experienced from it, you can see that despite their rich heritage, millions of Christians cannot see God's purpose for apostles. As a result, many of them do not reap this office's benefits, although they are bountiful. If you are going to become a quality, Apostolic Christian, you will need to know why this minister is essential to the Lord's Great Commission. You will have to gain His perspective on the gospels and become intimately familiar with the work of the Holy Spirit. In depth answers to these and other concerns is the King of kings' apostles' specialty. Straightforwardly, they tell you what God actually says on the matters affecting your Christianity from the Almighty's vantage point. It is not enough to hear what someone else says He feels about His conflict with the spirit and culture of this world. You must know for yourself what He judges as good, what He condemns as evil, and His reasons for deciding one or the other. This is particularly important if you are going to become a strong defender of His faith.

Take time as a group to hammer out solutions to apostleship's hindrances as you now understand them.

Outline what you know about apostleship's struggle to be accepted, and some ways discipling Apostolic Christians can relieve a large part of it.

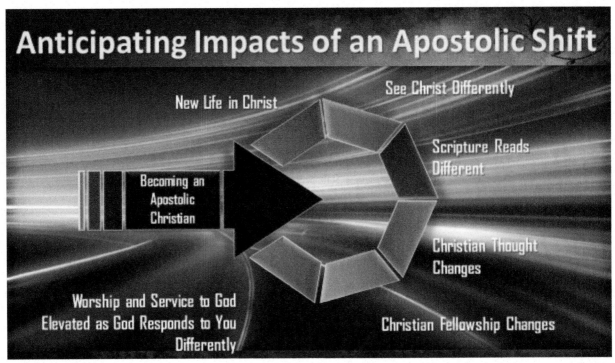

Before moving on in our discussion, take a moment to think through all that has been said so far and biblically verify what has just been said with what is written in 1 Peter 2:9; Revelation 1:6 and 5:10.

Final Thoughts

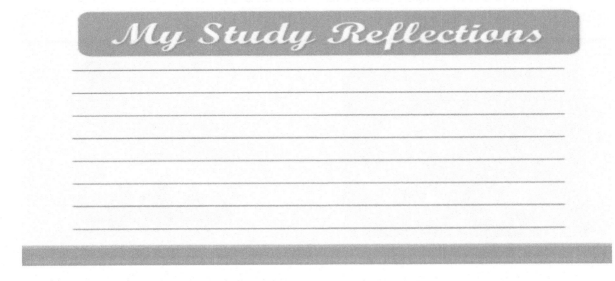

God Has Specific & Peculiar Reasons for Apostleship

In respect to the apostles' value to the body of Christ[19], 1 Corinthians 12:28 and Ephesians 4:11 along with Ephesians 2:20 make the Lord's point. Acts 2:42-47; 4:32-35; 5:12-16 and Acts 26:18 all make cover it. The Acts references underscore the wisdom of 1 Corinthians 12:28 & 29 as they set God's order the best. Look at the sequence—1st apostles, 2nd prophets, 3rd teachers, 4th miracle workers, 5th healings, 6th helps, 7th governments, 8th tongues. The evangelical church popularized the "nine gifts of the spirit", but apostleship which precedes it, lays out its "eight foundations" in 1 Corinthians 12:28, 29. The passage reinforces apostles and prophets as God's kingdom, and ecclesial cornerstones. Combine 1 Corinthians 12:28 and 29 together with Ephesians 4:11 and you see the church was founded on a threefold office foundation before it was served by the fivefold ministry gifts. The threefold is how apostleship settled and secured the church through its eight foundational powers.

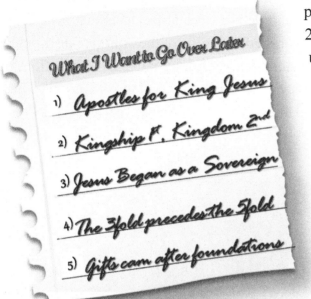

What I Want to Go Over Later

1) Apostles for King Jesus

2) Kingship 1st, Kingdom 2nd

3) Jesus Began as a Sovereign

4) The 3fold precedes the 5fold

5) Gifts cam after foundations

The Gifts (Manifestations) of the Spirit

It should be said here that what is traditionally called the "nine gifts of the spirit", spelled out in 1 Corinthians 12:7-11, are in fact not presented in the epistle as *gifts* at all. Paul never uses the word translated 'gifts' to identify them but rather a word that we would today translate as *phantom* or something akin to it. The original term for the nine actions listed in 1 Corinthians 12:7-11 is not "gifts" of the Spirit, but rather "manifestations" of the Spirit. As you can see, there is a big difference between the two terms that could lay to rest some of the commotion surrounding their ministerial practice. The way the Holy Spirit manifested to deliver His blessings to the Lord's church was characterized as 'phantomic' by Paul. As a ghost, His leave behind effects of knowledge, wisdom, prophecy, healings, discernment, and such (in Paul's mind), all fell under the heading of what a ghost-like phantom would do. Except in case of God's Spirit, the people were not terrified or taunted but healed and delivered, and informed and counseled.

---

[19] Conduct an extensive scripture study of the scriptures used here.

About the Holy Spirit's Manifestations

A phantomic manifestation is a showing forth of something, better yet someone, who is otherwise invisible and his or her effects usually indiscernible. The person manifesting uses spectacularity to announce his or her presence and deliver special products that benefit the audience. This explains why Paul declared the so-called nine gifts of the Spirit are <u>distributed,</u> as the Spirit wills. They are not granted by human initiatives but by the predeterminations of the Holy Spirit who at times using a human vessel to exercise and accomplish His will. Thus, the dynamisms displayed operate as His personal manifestations. Hence, what the Lord does

by His Spirit is to be separated from the ministry and the spiritual gifts He endows others to perform for Him. The Holy Spirit's manifestations, misnomered gifts, must come from something, and that something is identified in the last part of Paul's epistle to the Corinthians. They come from the eight foundations named above. From its governors to its ecclesial communications, the order is clear. Apostles ignite and launch, prophets declare and confirm, and teachers educate and disciple. These are the principal spiritual operatives of the New Creation church. The ecclesia's primal powers are: a) miracles (really miracle workers[20]), b) healings, c) helps d) governments, e) celestial tongues[21]. Collectively, these uphold the Lord Jesus' true ecclesia, supplying and sustaining its existence.

Once the above order is in place, the least known member of the staff emerges, the miracle worker. The appearance and operation of this minister positions the Lord's divinely ordained corps of ministers to serve His church on earth. The church ministers' right alignment, as specified by God, enables the ecclesia to function according to its heavenly model. When divine order is set, the healings begin because it takes healed people to become the healthy

---

[20] Miracles and miracle workers are distinguished by the acts and the performers. These are not miracles that the Holy Spirit arbitrarily performs, but miracle acts that are performed by a particular class of ministers endued with the special power to do so with the same discretionary latitude as the preacher, prophet or other servant of God.
[21] 1 Corinthians 13:1, "Though I speak with the tongues of men and of angels, and have not charity, I am become as sounding brass, or a tinkling cymbal."

helpers that manage the church's growth, and from them, the governors that prudently steer and regulate it.

When Things Are All in Order

When all kingdom and ecclesial structures are in order, then their providences can function synergistically on earth. The long closed channel that permits intercommunications between God's world and this one reopens and becomes fully operable for Christians to hear from their Redeemer. A once clogged heavenly portal now streams God's communications to this world and allows Him to relate to His family and guide its superintendence of His earthly institutions. All of these actions are essential for the people of God to participate in

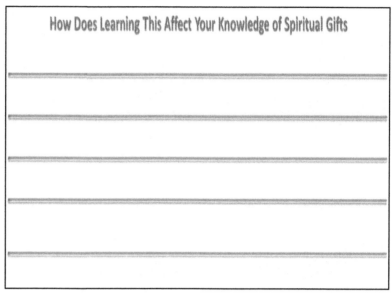

How Does Learning This Affect Your Knowledge of Spiritual Gifts

and enjoy the legacy, begun way back in time with Yahweh's first nation, Israel. Complete the following activities before reading further about our Israeli Legacy.

Applying It Today

Give 3 Present Day Revelations that You Would Classify as Strictly Apostolic. Share Them With Your Study Group.	

SCRIPTURE R.E.M.I.N.D.E.R. EXERCISE

"Let this mind be in you, which was also in Christ Jesus..." Philippians 2:5

Scripture Study: **Revelation - Explanation - Mysteries - Insight - Need - Demonstration - Example - Relevance**

Put some thought into the scripture(s) and respond to them according to the R.E.M.I.N.D.E.R. Exercise: 1 Corinthians 12:3-7, 28-29 as contrasted with Ephesians 4:11 and Acts 6:3.

Revelation

Explanation

Mysteries

Insight

Need

Demonstration

Example

Relevance

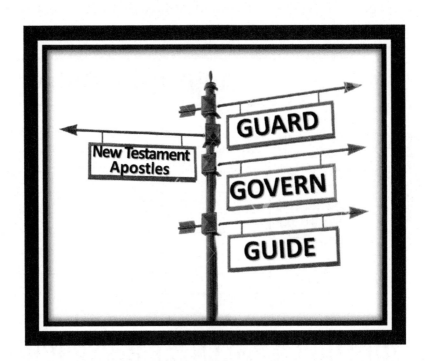

M.I.N.D. the Word Activity

"For who hath known the mind of the Lord, that he may instruct him? But we have the mind of Christ." 2 Corinthians 2:16

The M.I.N.D. the Word Activity seeks to guide your personal use of the scriptures in your daily life. It gives you the opportunity to fuse the passage's wisdom with your soul. Allow it to instruct you on the behaviors that you feel you need corrected to properly fulfill your duty to God's truth in action.

Scripture:

Motive: Why did God include it in His Bible?

Answer:

Instruction: What does God want to teach you from this passage?

Lesson:

Necessity: What about your beliefs or behaviors make this passage necessary for you?

Issue:

Duty: What must you do to observe, conform to, and practice this word every day?

Change:

Reinforcement Exercise

After your reading and scripture study exercise, develop and implement a mock workshop to prepare yourselves to use this information to attract or fortify Apostolic Christians. You will repeat this exercise later in the training.

Processing Reading With Your Discussion Group

WHAT	ask for information about something.
WHEN	ask about the time that something happened or will happen.
WHERE	ask questions about place or position.
WHICH	ask for information about one of a limited number of things
WHO	ask about someone's identity
WHOM	ask about the object (person) in the sentence
WHOSE	ask about possession.
WHY	ask for the reason
HOW	ask about the way in which something is done.

Visualizing What to Do With Your Responses

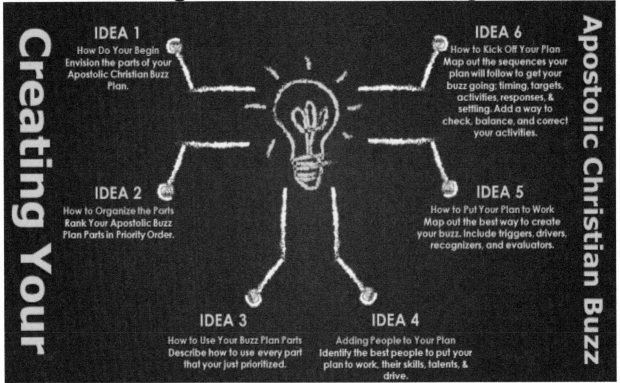

Idea Points for Above Chart

1.

2.

3.

4.

5.

6.

UNIT 5

Our Israeli Legacy

This unit is especially powerful in that it brings awakening Apostolic Christians into the heart of why the Lord wants them to transition to this branch of Christianity. The material to come exposes the relentless battle Christianity has with the "Gates of Hell. It does so by confronting what disturbs many of you today about the world, Jesus' true church, and the hostile treatment of your King and His kingdom.

Almighty God's church, kingdom, and faith are all under vicious attack. His people are at a loss for what to do, being caught in the grip of the "love and never judge" theology that binds them from acting or responding decisively to ungodly threats. With that come the opposers of our faith demanding we modernize Christianity by converting to their deities' culture. The full scale assault

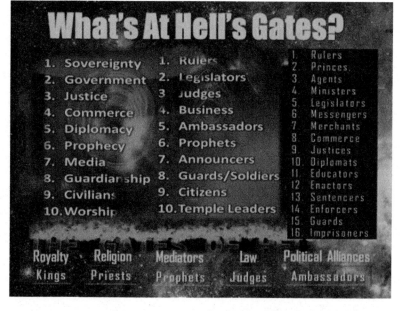

wants us to abandon our duty to our God and His salvation to serve sin rather than to protect His truth. And it does not stop there because we must also decide as Christians whether to just go on winning souls and leave their sanctification and the security of Christ's church up to Him. Or do we expand our evangelistic mandate to include guarding our Savior's worldwide progress. These are but a few of the pressing issues facing us today and the answer to them is stepping up to become an Apostolic Christian, to continue soul winning, and also engage in soul warring and Christian recovery at the same time. Before you collapse into overwhelmed panic know that God has been here before and has always triumphed. Take Joshua and Gideon's eras as examples. Here is the situation.

If you are like most Christians, you may have realized that the Lord's church is caught somewhere between the "Post Joshua Era", a generation of people who do not know the Lord[22]

and the "Gideon Era" where His signs, wonders, and miracles have become mere urban legends. In both instances, God had withdrawn from His people and no longer answered or provided for them, which brought the reality of His historical feats into question. His silence made verifying His miraculous power impossible and caused His people to lapse into unbelief [23] as a result. The situation is not too dissimilar today.

In the wake of today's relentless assaults on His Son and His church, it appears the Lord could not be more out of touch or disinterested in what is taking place on earth. Rest assured however, that He is very in touch and working behind the scenes to implement His responses to our battles.

God is never idle and is presently preparing in secret to do what He has always done. That is, to recover His people and rescue His church from the Gates of Hell. This subject is very important to you who are embarking upon Apostolic Christianity. What makes it important is the customary way God's adversaries shut Him out of His world and its government. In fact, all seven spheres of human civilization bar Him. Quickly for ease of memorization, these are summed up as 1) Religion, 2) Family, 3) Government, 4) Education, 5) Entertainment, 6) Business, and 7) Defense. You may know them as the seven mountains of culture, but I see them more precisely as spheres of domain since much of the world's power is no longer rustic, nor are its 21st dominators countrified mountaineers.

---

[22] Joshua 24:31; Judges 2:10.
[23] Judges 6:13.

Modern civilizations' mountains are today's corporate towers and their domains spherically (and subtly spiritually) defined. A development that appears to be something anticipated by the Apostle Paul based on his language in 2 Corinthians 10:12-16. Back then, he saw the world being increasing populated by metropolitan cities and less by villages. Underdeveloped nations are still this way with the natural mountains being their greatest challenge outside of survival. But long before Christ's time village dwellers were fast becoming city people with nations forming alliances drawn by political boundaries and no longer geographic ones.

A biblical example of a neo nation's progression to statehood is Israel's birth in the wilderness. After being delivered from Egypt, the new nation met its liberating God in the wilderness. There, they were brought to Yahweh's mountain to meet their new stronghold and to conform to their new theocratic government. The entire Exodus ordeal had taken them from a city-based civilization to a wilderness family of clans. As time went on however, they developed into a powerful state. Eventually Moses' portable wilderness tabernacle gave way to Solomon's stationary temple and God's mountaintop capital, the City of David with Mount Zion as His fortress. The new temple housed the once tabernacled Ark of the Covenant concealed in the holy of holies. Whichever you prefer, recognize from this example that God ordained His ecclesia to dominate every mountain or sphere of His world in His name. It seems He had more than soul winning in view when He spoke about the Gates of Hell not prevailing against His church.

The Sovereign Savior envisioned ongoing international discipleship. Then the gates were little more than frontages of their cities' walls. Today, those gates represent something else that only Jesus back then fully understood. They not only symbolized the seven spheres of domain or the seven mountains if you prefer, but also reminisced His eternal struggles with their spiritual founders. Either way, the point is made, hell stalks God's church, and you and I must become adept at resisting its stratagems.

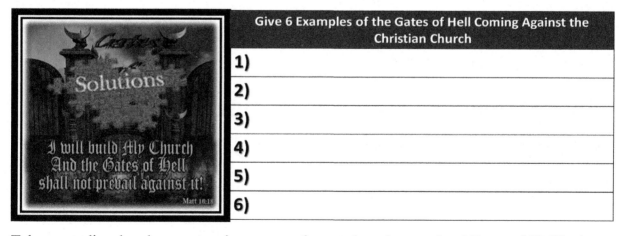

	Give 6 Examples of the Gates of Hell Coming Against the Christian Church
1)	
2)	
3)	
4)	
5)	
6)	

Take a reading break now to give some of your thoughts on the "Gates of Hell" above.

Afterward, you can opt to hold a training lab with your group to dig deeper into the ancient passage to discover how so much relevance it has today. Resume your reading to learn how God rescues His people when you have completed your group exercises.

How God Rescues His People

Historically, to implement His solutions and to rescue His people, the Lord raised up prophets to do it for Him; as was His way in natural Israel. Today, He uses apostles in a similar, but broader manner under the church age. These are two more reasons you need them in your life and in the modern world. The very same issues that plagued natural Israel in the past, today stalks the Lord Jesus' church. This sure word comes from our contemporary times mirroring the Lord's eternal and ancient ones. We are dealing with the same God, the same devil, and the same Adamic humans. All three cause the same cycle of circumstances to crop up repeatedly to try the saints and to prove the Almighty's majesty in every age.

To stave off Satan's endless onslaughts, the Lord revives and commissions modern apostles to resume what their predecessors began. That is, to defend His faith, to guard His flock, and to secure His kingdom. Guardianship is at the very center of apostles' work and those called to be Apostolic Christians understand it.

Other Reasons to Embrace Biblical Apostleship

Here are a few more situations, that motivate God, to send His apostles to resolve for Him. I call them Satan's top ten fiendish stratagems of the "Gates of Hell.

1. The church chose new gods
2. Christ's enemy is at the gates
3. Satanism and false prophets

4. The doctrines of devils
5. The commandments of men
6. Seducing Spirits
7. Spiritual Warfare
8. Apostasy
9. Assaults on the Lord and His Christ
10. Cultural competition for Christian faith

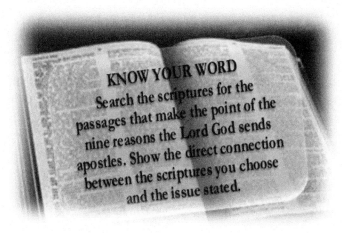

KNOW YOUR WORD
Search the scriptures for the passages that make the point of the nine reasons the Lord God sends apostles. Show the direct connection between the scriptures you choose and the issue stated.

Take a moment now to relate the ten stratagems to the malicious legislation the world is enacting against the modern church of the Lord Jesus Christ. Pull current events items from the news to make your connections and prove your point. Discuss what should be the Christian response to The Ten Reasons to Embrace Apostleship. Present your response in a comparison between apostleship and evangelicalism as you now detect it, then pick up your reading with Apostles in Action.

After Reading Assignment

Develop 5 Reading Comprehension Questions!

And Then

RESEARCH Examples of **MALICIOUS LEGISLATION AGAINST THE CHURCH**

Apostles in Action

What many Christians do not know about apostleship is that, among other things, God raises up apostles under the church's dispensation to fulfill the vow He makes in Matthew 16:18. He deploys them to keep the "Gates of Hell" from prevailing against His ecclesia. To this end, He commissions and dispatches apostles and prophets to extend Jesus' kingship into this world. They impose His realm's security and purity on this one. Thus, apostleship serves a more pervasive kingdom role than an ecclesial one. Its royal duties take precedence over its ecclesial ones because it originated under a monarchy and not a church ministry.

Give a little thought to all that has just been said and process it through the following activity.

ACTIVE READING EXERCISE
Notes, Questions, Discoveries

Review what you just read and think about how you would: a) Share it with others, b) use it to teach, c) transform your Christian walk, and d) persuasively respond to questions, disputes, or debates.

WRITE A RELEVANT QUESTION	ANSWER YOUR RELEVANT QUESTION

WRITE A RELATED ISSUE	RESPOND TO YOUR RELATED ISSUE

WRITE A SCENARIO	ANSWER YOUR SCENARIO

RELATE A SCRIPTURE	CONNECT YOUR RELATED SCRIPTURE

SUGGEST A TEACHING IDEA	DESCRIBE YOUR TEACHING IDEA

Reinforcement Activity

GROUP
Discussion

Session

Focus _____

1. _____
2. _____
3. _____
4. _____

Spend time talking about what you just learned. Exchange thoughts on it and suggest some ideas about how to put it to use in your world.

More Apostleship in Action

Apostleship furthermore manifests as a collaborative that functions somewhere between a franchise and an embassy, because of the special partnership that forms between the apostle and the Lord as their Sender. When you think of the apostles' Sender (and them His Sent ones) remember the opening definition of apostleship. Do not forget that God makes His apostles, His stand-ins on earth. The office's ancient attributes endue modern apostles to collaborate with Christ on His global commission in a proprietary[24] way. Together the two, embassy and commission, define the civilization side of Jesus' divine mandate, which is to bring His Father's sons and daughters home. To accomplish His aim, the most fundamental subject the Savior needs His apostles to adopt and then spread is His full life story. They should become well versed in His power to save, sanctify, deliver, and prosper those who come to God through

---

[24] Look up this word and relate its meanings to apostleship.

Him, according to Hebrews 7:25. Apostles of the Lion of Judah are obliged to immerse themselves in the Almighty's world without end relocation plan. A plan that He implemented long before this world was. That plan is the nexus of the Christian's redemption.

An Apostle Is "A sovereign's sent one."

God's Long Standing Relocation Plan

From the beginning, the Creator planned to relocate those born to Adam and born again in Christ to His world. Notice the use of the word 'relocate' because its use is deliberate since Christianity is the Creator's first civilization. His plan forms the lynchpin of the Apostles' Doctrine mentioned in the Book of Acts, and shapes the messages that come from apostles' mouths. Reconciling this simple sounding venture may be considered the height of why God maintains the apostle's office. It is key to understanding the eternal origins and moorings of Christianity. Therefore, the first step every one of Christ's commissioned apostles must take is to decide the way they will represent the Son of God as the eternal King of kings and God of gods. That step comprehensively begins with what began (took and takes place) in heaven, not with what is carried out on earth.

As a first step, the apostle's commission process starts with the King of kings proving Himself to be alive, and His world indisputably being in charge of this one. To earn the privilege of representing the Lord, genuine apostles' ministry careers are launched with a face-to-face encounter with the resurrected Jesus Christ. Think about what all of that involves and then do the Active Reading Exercise below. Work through it inspired by what you just read. Complete this exercise based on what you learned. After finishing the exercise, resume your reading to learn about apostle's encounter with the Risen Christ.

ACTIVE READING EXERCISE

RELATE A SCRIPTURE	CONNECT YOUR RELATED SCRIPTURE

WRITE ANOTHER QUESTION	ANSWER YOUR QUESTION

SUGGEST A TEACHING IDEA	DESCRIBE YOUR TEACHING IDEA

The Risen Christ & Apostleship Commission

Taking that first apostleship step brought me into the encounters and experiences with the Risen Lord Jesus Christ. Those early divine episodes also delivered my commission to me. Divine interactions with the Savior illuminated me on what backs and propels my call to apostleship. That framework drives my apostleship, and influences my hope for your use of this material and your future as an Apostolic Christian. Ideally, you will use it to identify the Apostolic Christians the Lord assigns to His apostolic leaders. With sage insight, you will be able to teach your church and ministry members about their Christianity from its origins and to reveal their Savior's intents for their soul's salvation. Attempting to teach Christianity apart from exposing your learners to their apostolic roots is only half the job. Comprehensive training must go from history to destiny. How it all began should shape what is to be a training's expected end. For your learners to get the most out of your teachings, share your training in a way that will <u>arm</u> and not just <u>inform</u> them.

Before you set out to teach this to others however, review all of the scripture references given so far to design your class around what you learn here. Whenever I have done so, I have seen God's people grow stronger and more convinced of why theirs is indeed the one true faith in all the world. After your review, write out some of the persuasive ways you plan to discuss, and if need be, defend your faith in Jesus Christ using what you now know and understand about it. Afterward, we look at what makes Christianity superior to every other faith.

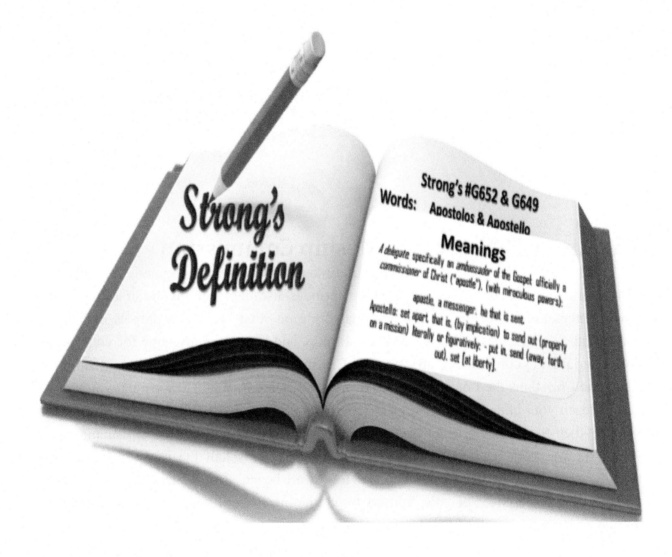

Strong's #G652 & G649

Words: Apostolos & Apostello

Meanings

A delegate, specifically an ambassador of the Gospel, officially a commissioner of Christ ("apostle"), (with miraculous powers):

apostle, a messenger, he that is sent.

Apostello: set apart, that is, (by implication) to send out (properly on a mission) literally or figuratively: - put in, send (away, forth, out), set [at liberty].

Come up with some good discussion points about Apostolic Christianity using this card's explanations.	
WHAT	ask for information about something.
WHEN	ask about the time that something happened or will happen.
WHERE	ask questions about place or position.
WHICH	ask for information about one of a limited number of things
WHO	ask about someone's identity
WHOM	ask about the object (person) in the sentence
WHOSE	ask about possession.
WHY	ask for the reason
HOW	ask about the way in which something is done.

Christians' Superior Premise

If you are a Christian, by now you know that being one sets you in an unusual class, spiritually speaking when it comes to religions and worship. There was a time when that class was celebrated, but now it is often condemned. If you are not trying to conform your New Creation redemption to the religions of this world, you are learning every day, that belonging to Christ is not without its scuffles or its adversaries.

Living in this world as "not of it" proves that Christianity's markers are unlike those of any other religion. The reason it is not has to do with six identifiers that define (and distinguish) every religion: They are 1) each religion's founder, 2) the invisible power that converted and backs the founder, 3) the source and cause of the faith a religion spreads, 4) the location that birthed a particular religion, 5) how a religion makes its converts, and 6) the afterlife promises and performances of the faith. These six factors are important because they draw the line that separates (and elevates) Christianity above the other religions of this world. Christianity makes no sense to this world because how this world got its start escapes, or is rejected by many of its inhabitants. Attempting to separate how the world began from the one that began it keeps the cycle of questions and speculations that puzzles most human seekers going. That frustrating cycle carries over to those attempting to comprehend Christianity, because it and this world share the same source origins. Thus, their answers

TAKE ACTION Develop 5 Reading Comprehension Questions!

disclose our faith as the real deal, because to accept "In the beginning God" is to accept "In the beginning was the word" and that "The Word became flesh." Based on these two premises, the main dynamic that distinguishes our faith is its most compelling one, its origins. Christianity began before this world was made and this world was made by Christianity's Founder.

What you just read is powerful and should be considered carefully, so pause your reading for a moment to reflect on what has just been said and what it means (and says) to you. Note your insights to these and resume your reading with what makes Christianity not of this world and why it is necessary for you as Christ's convert to know it.

What It Says & Means To Me

1) _____

2) _____

3) _____

4) _____

5) _____

6) _____

7) _____

9) _____

We Really Are Not of This World

Christianity is not of this world, because its Founder the Maker of all things did not come from here. Ephesians 3:9 frankly asserts this truth. Christ being from another world is a peculiarity that should inspire you who are His to think beyond the norm and the obvious at the same time. As you mature, Christianity moves you to do just that and to do something else that is otherwise impossible. It drives you to learn to live jointly in this world and God's at once. When you do, you simultaneously transcend time and space and still remain time and earth bound to both in this world. What a masterful capacity; if only we could just grab hold of it. What a majestic privilege; if only we could wrap our heads and hearts around it.

5 Things That Make Christianity Not of This World

1. _____

2. _____

3. _____

4. _____

5. _____

Perhaps what is to come will help you do both. It is now time for you to understand what heaven and earth really are to God and Christ, and how your redemption is at the heart and soul of their created purposes. The next section tells you how Christianity got to earth.

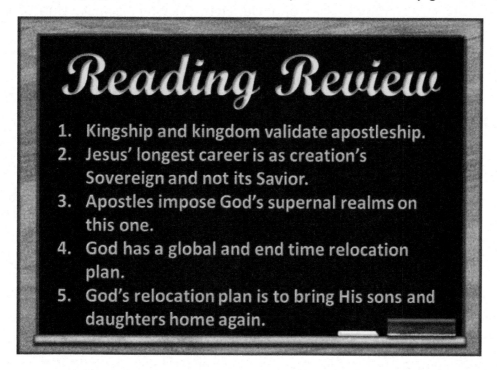

Reading Review

1. Kingship and kingdom validate apostleship.
2. Jesus' longest career is as creation's Sovereign and not its Savior.
3. Apostles impose God's supernal realms on this one.
4. God has a global and end time relocation plan.
5. God's relocation plan is to bring His sons and daughters home again.

UNIT 6

Heaven on Earth

Christianity was brought from heaven to earth the day the Holy Spirit baptized the 120 in the upper room, see Luke 24:49 and Acts 1:13. His arrival on earth that Pentecost did more than just instill His presence within Christians' beings; it also installed the Creator's eternity in our world. Our eternal beginnings make Christianity as the Godhead designed and implemented it sound way too sci-fi to be trusted, let alone embraced. Yet it is precisely what it is, and also it is why it does exactly what it implies. Heaven came to earth within the body of a human being, and through that human being, it is invisibly populating itself the same way.

Source of Apostolic Doctrine
THE PROPHETS
Jesus Taught the Prophets
His Apostles Taught the Prophets
Making Apostolic Christians Are Also Prophetic

Extending God's world into this one is the truth that isolates Christianity from every other religion on earth. In fact, ours is not a religion at all, but a divine colony occupied by spirits, redeemed from the earth by the blood of Jesus Christ. Embedding Himself within the souls of those that believe in Him annexes[25] this world to His. In the process, He uses the acts described above to bring the Apostolic Christian back into eternal life while still on earth. Later that same power transports the redeemed in Christ back to His world in the end.

---

[25] Look up this word to realize what the Lord actually did for us and how it affects our place in His world.

How It All Happened

During the Savior's day when He revealed heaven's salvation objectives and the outcomes of His incarnation, crucifixion, and resurrection, Jesus' explanation made sense to those who heard Him. That era did not find His revelations too foreign because He spoke in terms of the then world. Using metaphors that speak of land and population conquests, Jesus shrewdly made His point by using widespread ambassadorial and territorial conflicts and conquests to compare with His pending salvation's eternal effect.

Reaching beyond faith and belief, Christianity's Founder accomplished the unthinkable. He incorporated those entering His body into the Godhead's divine lineage, an idea that Nicodemus in John chapter 3 found difficult to perceive. See also Ephesians chapter 3:1-19 for further corroboration. The rabbinical teacher's unbelief aside; that is what the Savior of the world, Israel's Messiah did then and what He continues to do today. Daily, Christ Jesus reabsorbs His converts into His body, swapping their Adamic genes for His own, to make them wholly embodied citizens of His heavenly home.

Next, we decode the Christian's Godhead genus. Before we do though, answer the following questions and discuss as a study group: **Activity**: Answer the following, discuss as a study group, and then read about how it all happened:

1) **How did Christianity get to earth?**

2) **What tripped Nicodemus up?**

3) **How does Jesus Christ make a Christian?**

The Christian Genus

Christianity's principal distinctive is that Christians are born from God's patented divine stock. That is its secret formula and the source of its mysterious powers. Unlike every other human, Christians started life eternal. Long before we were planted on earth, we existed in Jesus Christ the first begotten Son of God. Our eternal preexistence qualified us to become His offspring.

To get us out of Adam's doomed lineage and back into Christ's, the Lord Jesus' Father begot us again made us born (anew) from above by the Holy Spirit. It is why Romans says if you "do not have His spirit you are not His." Those that cannot enter Christ's world when they die are denied because they were not in Him <u>before</u> the foundation of the world. Not being His in heaven when He lived as the Son of God is the reason why people cannot receive Jesus Christ's salvation in this world. Ephesians 1:4 makes this very point. Read 2 Timothy 1:9. To be saved, to hear God's call to repentance, is possible because of the promise God made Jesus His first begotten before the world began[26]. Apostolic Christians can really relate to this because of their instinctual sense of the world above this one, and the strange inkling that they are and somehow were always a part of it.

Not belonging to Jesus Christ refers to being devoid of His Holy Spirit within. God is faithful to His Son's seed and as promised sets in motion the processes what will return them to their original estate when they leave this world. The guarantee of that promise is our embodiment of the Spirit of the Lord Jesus Christ, the portion of the Holy Spirit that incorporates and extends the second person of the Godhead.

Christianity is foremost being reinserted in Jesus Christ's being to rejoin His immortal family. Invisible to the naked eye, that insignificant sounding "sinner's prayer" kick starts a highly advanced, completely divine, technological process. From there, repentance and redemption go to work to repatriate Christ's converts in His celestial world as fully developed humans. Imagine it, something as simple as the "sinner's prayer" naturalizes us as everlasting citizens of God's eternal kingdom. It does that is, when the repentance is genuine. Think on these points for a moment and jot your thoughts down in the ROAD to Apostolic Christianity card below.

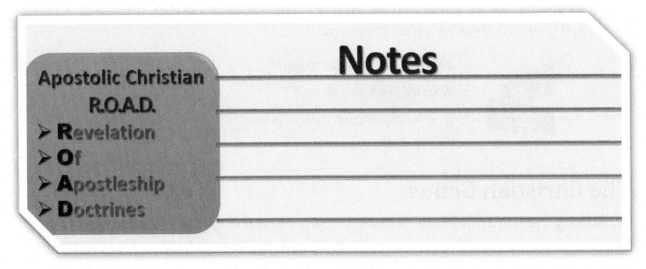

Apostolic Christian R.O.A.D.
➢ **R**evelation
➢ **O**f
➢ **A**postleship
➢ **D**octrines

Notes

In effect, simply acknowledging and confessing your sins to the Lord with a sincere heart stops your mortality and makes you an immortal replica of Jesus the Messiah and the rest of the Godhead. Nothing could qualify more as the seeming foolishness of God than this. His eternal life method is so nonsensical that it escapes the unbeliever while making perfect sense to those who were in Christ before this world was. To assure that only those in His family return home, the Almighty makes evangelism and repentance ridiculous to the prideful so they reject Him.

---

[26] See Titus 1:2.

As odd as it seems, the unbeliever's rejection serves the Lord's spiritual recovery and relocation plan perfectly. See 1 Peter 2:9.

ACTIVE READING EXERCISE

Relate a Scripture	Connect Your Related Scripture

Suggest a Teaching Idea	Describe Your Teaching Idea

GROUP Discussion

Session

How Does It Work?

Spend time as a group imagining how you would recognize the signs of apostleship in action from what you just read.

What Salvation Means

When Christian's mortal body returns to the dust, your soul and spirit are transported to God's world where they began. Only this time they enter it as a whole person, and not as the seed that you were when you left it. What a marvelous revelation. If you began above with Christ and not on the earth, at your death that is where you return. It is where you go if you believe His gospel and receive His salvation. If you fit the classification of those Jesus describes in Matthew 13, you cannot enter God's world because you lack the eternal equipment to do so.

On the other hand, an amazing heavenly destiny awaits you who are Christ's. That destiny is why God calls His Gospel His "Good News". The massive tragedy that took place in Eden to imprison us in this world was really a part of a masterful plan the Lord devised to free us from earth's death and re-implant us in Jesus Christ. His actions return us (spirit and soul) to where we began. Taking the awe-inspiring details of our faith at face value exposes why Christianity never qualified as a world religion. Its riddle is solved when you realize that it is and has always been the mysterious part of the Creator's everlasting civilization. It was <u>not</u> born on earth, but was transported to it. Consequently, it fails to meet the qualifications of a world religion and the world's constant assaults on it attest to this daily.

Strong's Definition

Strong's #5449

Words: **Phusis**

From 2 Peter 1:4 -- Divine Nature

Meanings

Growth by germination or expansion, by implication, natural production, lineal descent; a genus...

M.I.N.D. the Word Activity

"For who hath known the mind of the Lord, that he may instruct him? But we have the mind of Christ." 2 Corinthians 2:16

The M.I.N.D. the Word Activity seeks to guide your personal use of the scriptures in your daily life. It gives you the opportunity to fuse the passage's wisdom with your soul and then allow it to instruct you on the behaviors that you feel you need corrected, to properly fulfill your duty to God's truth in action

Scripture: 1 Timothy 2:9; 1 Corinthians 2:7; Titus 1:2 (Collective Study)

Motive: <u>Why did God include it in His Bible?</u>

Answer:

Instruction: <u>What does God want to teach you from this passage?</u>

Lesson:

How Christians Go Back to God's First Civilization

As God's first civilization, Christians came to earth by way of the Holy Spirit, whom the Almighty poured out on Pentecost. Christ has always had custody of those who are born again from the Godhead. That is what the new birth actually means and does. As His seed, Jesus would have had the Christian in His being before He became the world's Messiah. Otherwise, how can we be His offspring? His receiving our repentance is not the first time He has been responsible for keeping us. We were embodied in the first begotten and maintained by Him in heaven before the earth was made; even then, we were the body of Christ. That origin means our redemption is a mystery not an earthly religion. A mystery the Holy Spirit finally divulges to God's people in Hebrews 12:22-24. Along with it, read what makes Jesus the Almighty's firstborn in Colossians 1:15-22. In light of all that has been said, you will find the two references interesting reading.

Pause now to complete the Active Reading Exercise and then read on in order to learn what all you just read means to the Lord and His Christian offspring.

ACTIVE READING EXERCISE
Notes, Questions, Discoveries

Write a Question	Answer Your Question

Relate a Scripture	**Connect Your Related Scripture**

Summarily, the Hebrews and Colossians passages you just read say well what it is that makes Christians the Almighty's superior progeny. They were in their Maker while He was still a King, before He became a Savior. Prior to the foundation of this world (or any world for that matter), Christians existed as Christ's seed, awaiting the New Creation to manifest fully as His siblings and offspring. That majestic fact defines what makes people Christian and nothing else. The supernal[27] acts and processes of Jesus' Father transformed Christ's offspring from dead seeds, to make them deathless immortals of His everlasting kingdom.

Activity: Answer the following and discuss as a study group:

1) What is Christianity's mystery power?

2) What is God's secret formula?

3) What do the scriptures referred to tell us about Christianity?

What It All Means

Being born of God's divine nature effectively assimilates those begotten again in Christ into the Godhead to make them members of its body. Repentance and faith in the Lamb of God procreatively[28] turns Christ's earthly believers into God's blood relatives. Real, though intangible natal[29] procedures and substances transform penitents into the literal body of Christ. Intangibility aside, the end product though entirely sublime, reclassifies His followers as His

---

[27] Being or coming from on high--of heaven or the world of the celestial--otherworldly. Superlatively good, exquisite, exalted. Located in a higher region, superior in position. Of or from that which is on high, divine or celestial as coming from the heavenly regions or world endued with a higher nature, or greater excellence than most humans did. (wordsmyth.com). Appointed to more than earthly powers or human excellence; situated above in the heavenlies.

[28] producing new life or offspring

[29] Biological genetics.

offspring. That is not to say that you should overlook what John 3:3-8 says about following Jesus. One must become more than one of His disciples[30]. The redeemed must become as He is[31] because it is not the mere followers of Christ that reenter His world, but those that become His literal replicas do. Re-depositing us into the Godhead was always meant to be, seeing as we were in His literal body when there was no world or earth.

In our pre incarnate life, before we were humans, we lived Christ's life inside Him as He lived it in heaven. We started our existence as eternal seed housed within the Son of God. When we were born in the flesh, we became mortal and doomed to die because death is what Adam's curse passed on to his seed.[32] This effect of Adam's transgression made everything in him doomed to die although it took years for his body, and it takes years for our bodies to return to the dust. What that means to those born in this world is that death resides in every man's seed and every woman's egg. . In respect to our Savior's incarnation the moment that the eternal

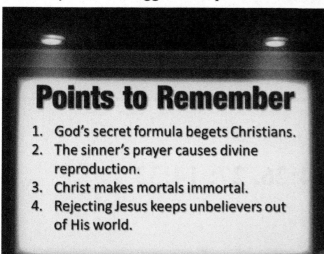

Points to Remember

1. God's secret formula begets Christians.
2. The sinner's prayer causes divine reproduction.
3. Christ makes mortals immortal.
4. Rejecting Jesus keeps unbelievers out of His world.

Christ entered Mary's womb He became a dead man and everything in Him died too. We were planted on earth to take on our bodies, because as said earlier, we began life as seeds and not people, so that we would be the exact image and likeness of our heavenly Father. So, regardless of how sad it sounds, God designed it that way to get us out of this planet's doom and back into His own world where we began life as seeds in His first begotten Son.

Our eternal nativity by the Godhead certifies our divine genetics, attested to and guarded by the Holy Spirit, who takes up residence within us. The Godhead's genes secure our birthright while the Holy Spirit as our passport authorizes our return to Christ's life. He assures we make it back home as mature offspring when we leave this world. The Holy Spirit is how we get back inside of God and Christ first and into their world last. Think of it, we began our existence within the body of Christ, and if we accept His free gift of salvation, we return there as fully-matured beings. Both actions regenerate us as the Messiah's immortal seed on the earth, and they immediately register us as citizens of heaven where the rest of His family resides. You see, monarchs' citizens are also their family, at least the first generation is.

---

[30] Luke 14:26, 27; 14:33.
[31] 1 John 4:17.
[32] 1 Corinthians 15:21, 22 – "In Adam all die."

Before studying the scriptures below, take a moment to write a reading review that states how this material helps Apostolic Christians and advances New Era Apostleship™.

Spend some time reviewing all that you just read. Challenge yourself by coming up with a few review questions that you would put to your training group of emerging or developing Apostolic Christians.

Scripture Study
Study Luke 14:26, 27; 14:33

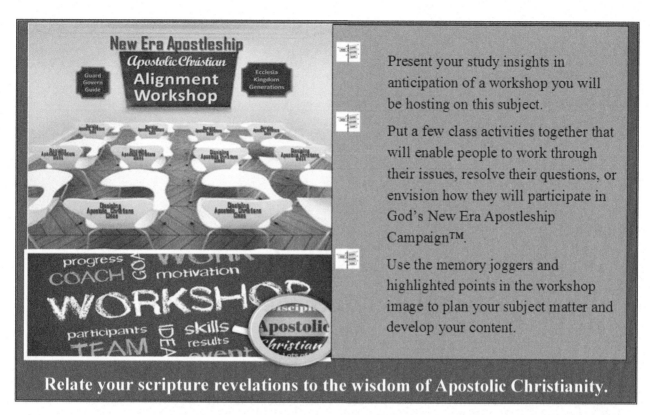

Present your study insights in anticipation of a workshop you will be hosting on this subject.

Put a few class activities together that will enable people to work through their issues, resolve their questions, or envision how they will participate in God's New Era Apostleship Campaign™.

Use the memory joggers and highlighted points in the workshop image to plan your subject matter and develop your content.

Relate your scripture revelations to the wisdom of Apostolic Christianity.

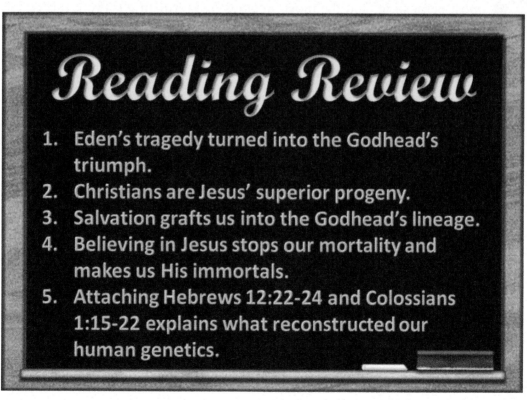

Reading Review

1. Eden's tragedy turned into the Godhead's triumph.
2. Christians are Jesus' superior progeny.
3. Salvation grafts us into the Godhead's lineage.
4. Believing in Jesus stops our mortality and makes us His immortals.
5. Attaching Hebrews 12:22-24 and Colossians 1:15-22 explains what reconstructed our human genetics.

UNIT 7

Secrets Kept Hidden Since the Foundation of the World

Among Christianity's deepest secrets, our genesis as the Godhead's offspring is the most perplexing, and the most precious one of them all. From the very beginning, the Almighty intended to reproduce Himself because He wanted a family. He placed us in His first begotten Son Jesus Christ to expedite the process of replicating Himself throughout all His worlds and endless ages.

As Creator, the Lord desires offspring from every being He makes, angels, humans, and only He knows what else. The way He as the Almighty determined to extract His family from the earth is through the blood of the cross and the lost soul's faith in it. A most profound mystery indeed, and there are many, many more like it to be discovered. Laying hold of the truths of our Creator lineage clarifies Christianity. His story is the taproot[33] of our God's truly transcendent mysteries. It is the stronghold of the Christian life and the basis for Christ's strong hold on us.

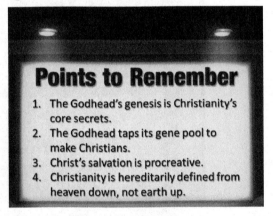

Points to Remember

1. The Godhead's genesis is Christianity's core secrets.
2. The Godhead taps its gene pool to make Christians.
3. Christ's salvation is procreative.
4. Christianity is hereditarily defined from heaven down, not earth up.

---

[33] Something that provides an important central source for growth or development; the central element or position in a line of growth or development, which penetrates the earth directly downward to a considerable depth without dividing. Figuratively, a "taproot" is the source of an idea or work. Onelookdictionary.com.

Amazingly, the Godhead's gene pool reproduces itself in the Christian's genetic code. It does so because the Lord never intended His children's conversion to Him to confine itself to convert faith alone, as is the case with other religions. Religions and faiths originating in this world come short of the supernal excellence of Christ's reproductive redemption, because they enroll their followers to enlist them their religion's faithfuls. They do not beget offspring, replicas of their deities. Christianity exists because God's Son passes on His genetics to the lost via the Holy Spirit. It is His divine lineage that defines the Christian.

All other spirit-to-worshippers' transactions require the spirit to enter the convert, not as it is with the born from above Christian. The Godhead's redemption brings its believers into its divine nature's genetics.

> "Whereby are given unto us exceeding great and precious promises: that by these ye might be partakers of the divine nature, having escaped the corruption that is in the world through lust."
>
> 2 Peter 1:4

That is another monumental difference that exalts Christianity above the world's fallen gods that only have the power to reproduce their nature in their believers as flesh and blood children under Adam's curse. Only their behaviors and manifestations are passed on and that one by one since they use the human reproductive system to invade Adam's seed and spawn their offspring. The Holy Spirit reproduces Christ en masse, meaning that He is replete with the Almighty's seed (usually called spores) to spread as much of Jesus as His offer of salvation demands. If 50,000 people come to Christ to be saved, then 50,000 New Creation spirits are dispensed to them all at once. In God, there is no shortage of new spirits and new hearts to go around, and it all happens in the blink of an eye. What fallen deities pass on is actually reinforces the mortality contained in the serpent until Adam surrendered to him. There is no spiritual procreation at all, since the power to give life is the Godhead's deepest mystery. The way we are saved, by being brought back into the body of Jesus Christ, makes ours a procreative salvation, not just a sentient[34] one. We get to live out a brand new nature aided by our new heart and spirit. Refer back to John 3:3-8 and Ezekiel 36:24-27.

Jesus' reproduction of Himself in His converts means the practice part of our Christian faith

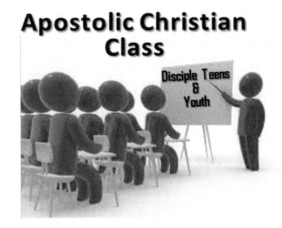

would be better understood as the outworking of our divine genealogy. For those in Christ Jesus, it is not just about believing in the Lord, it is entirely about "manifesting as His offspring". Reproducing lives that are just like His own expresses the overriding peculiarity of the Christian confidence to be found in John 1:12, 13. These are the disclosures that establish Christianity as much more than a religion; they make it supreme to all earthly religions.

Say how you would solve the problem of people questioning the reality of the new birth and the way you would explain it and validate it as a real experience. Lay out the points of discussion and persuasion that would best convince a Christian that we all began our life in Christ apostolically.

So Much More Than Emotional Faith

Faith is the Christian's highway to eternity. Moreover, for the reasons given above, Christianity qualifies as a nationality because of how its members are brought into existence,

---

[34] Emotional, conscious, sentimental, feeling one.

much of which you have learned already. Our faith is not a mere ethereal appliance that connects the spiritually hungry with otherworldly beings. For Christians, especially apostolic ones, faith in faith is just not enough. We need a person with the power to back our faith who quicken us daily to live above this world's mortality and corruption. Worldly faiths in comparison depict and promote hollow beliefs in an impersonal ideal. Christianity does not. It is hereditarily defined and that from heaven down, not earth up. Its authenticity and authority could never survive on worship and religious systems alone; no matter how elaborate they may be. Christianity is a person. It is not just faith in a person as a divine being. Christians are in person what they worship, not just worshippers of a faith. Beyond embodying Jesus Christ, their faith's Founder, those born again in Him carry the literal substance of His eternal godhood in flesh. In effect, Christian faith sends its converts back to a world that reaches eons beyond this one and engages its believers in the business heaven transacts on earth. Therefore, what it conveys are not repetitive routines, but the incarnation of its Founder, multiplied exponentially. God uses Christian worship forms merely to portray His invisible attributes and to depict the subtle manifestations that reveal and characterize His nature and culture.

Ritualistic rules can never do justice to the vessels of God's new creature in Jesus Christ; because Christians, as Jesus' supernal progeny, make up the Almighty's invisible and so humanly untraceable family on earth. His family is in this world to model Him and His lifestyle, and to attract the rest of the souls God ordained to salvation before the foundation of the world. Visible Christian faith in practice, is designed to convince our yet to be born again brothers and sisters to return to their heavenly origins, and to prove God's majesty to the invisible creatures that observe His doings in this world. This is what Ephesians 3:10 is referring to when it speaks of the principalities and powers in the heavenly places that are convinced of God's manifold wisdom by what the Savior's church does on earth.

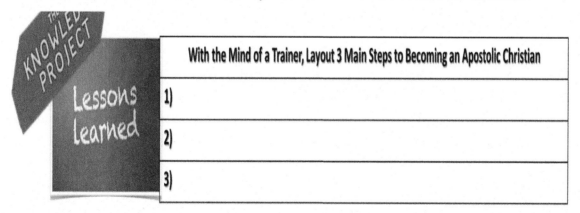

With the Mind of a Trainer, Layout 3 Main Steps to Becoming an Apostolic Christian
1)
2)
3)

The following passages of scripture say as much, study them to get a picture how the word of God voices what you just read as His truths. **Suggestion**: Spend time studying the scripture references and answer the following as a class:

John 3:31	John 8:23	Luke 16:8	John 18:36	Matthew 13:35	Matthew 25:34	Mark 10:33
Luke 1:70	John 10:36	John 15:19	John 16:28	John 17:5	John 17:9	John 17:16
John 17:18	John 17:24	Acts 3:21	Romans 16:25	2 Corinthians 2:7	2 Timothy 1:9	Titus 1:2
Hebrews 1:6	Hebrews 6:5	Hebrews 10:5	1 Peter 1:20	Revelation 13:8	Revelation 17:8	Ephesians 3:10

Activity: Now that you have completed your lengthy scripture study, answer these questions about what you just learned. Then you can move on to learn how to live the Godhead's life.

1. What do all scriptures have in common?
2. What do scriptures say about your salvation?
3. What is to be learned about your Christianity from the scriptures?

Living the Godhead's Life

Springing from the Godhead's family tree is the mystery of the Christian experience. All that underpins it evidences what Jesus did to pass us from death to life, not for humanity to upstage or sabotage its effects of His sovereignty. Religious rituals are the regimens the King of kings imposes on His family to enable our invisible state to be detected and manifested in the physical world. Both map out the Godhead's ideal way of practicing its culture on earth. Consequently, the church's forms and observances aim to attract to the rest of God's family, not to compete with those of His doomed gods. Those being born again are ordained to populate the Savior's kingdom on earth so they to flourish in His world later when it comes to earth.

Christian habits and observances help you discover and live out your kingdom destiny until your New Creation being reenters God's world. That is why His worship, services, and sacrifices do not change and typically run against the grain of earthly rituals. Of all the things they are to accomplish, the main one is that they are to sanctify us so we reflect the heavenly community we hope to join one day. If there were a second to that first, it would be to make a public difference between who belongs to the true and living God and who does not. Consequently, conforming our faith expressions to earth's deities demotes Christianity and promotes God's adversaries. The reason is that the way the Holy Spirit inspires us to express our faith in and love for God is not ancient, it is eternal. God's worship originated in heaven and His kingdom has been practicing its union with its God, His way, for eternities. Everything the Lord demands of us in the flesh is consistent with how His invisible creation keeps going and keeps in good stead with Him. Frankly speaking, it is their edge over the rebel spirits that were once their citizens, their former countrymen so to speak. Imposing their lifestyle on us, while we remain on earth, tutors us on living forever as supernal beings. Meanwhile, we get to perfect our eternal selves by using our New Creation life to access and appropriate the powers of God's "age to come", as the epistle to the Hebrews call it. Doing things our God's way strengthens our Christianity and enables us to enrich the people of this world.

Until that age comes however, Christians are to preserve their inheritance and to benefit their world. As a result, their presence on earth is to prosper the Messiah's kingdom and secure their eternal citizenship for as long as they are in the planet. These they do not only with doctrine but also with deeds that exemplify how life in heaven is lived. How does the Christian accomplish all this? By showing God's goodness, and by spreading on earth the exclusive providences He holds in His heavenly treasuries. The reason we do it is to aid earth's residents and to be

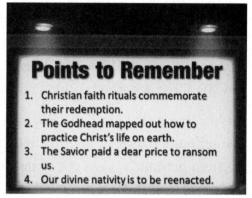

Points to Remember

1. Christian faith rituals commemorate their redemption.
2. The Godhead mapped out how to practice Christ's life on earth.
3. The Savior paid a dear price to ransom us.
4. Our divine nativity is to be reenacted.

God's light and salt in this world. Collectively, this sums up apostleship in action and how we evangelize others as Apostolic Christians. It is also how we persistently win the lost and disciple the nations beyond preaching.

Activity: Answer the following to discuss as a study group:

1) What is meant by "An Emotional Faith?"
2) Why is Christianity more than emotion?
3) How do you explain what you just read to 5 of your saved and 5 of your unsaved friends or associates?

Securing Our Heritage

Fully engaging in spreading Christ and His blessings in the world helps Christians remember that life under the sun is not all there is. It also guarantees they never forget that they, like their Founder, are not of this world. God desires His family to exude what made its Savior, creation's Sovereign, pay such a dear price to ransom it from sin and death. He needs us to become acutely aware of and familiar with His struggle with the vicious gods bent on destroying His children, just because they are His. All this information explains God's ransom of your soul and says why you owe Him your life. You owe it to Jesus and His Father to make their dream of a family made entirely in their image and likeness, come true. That is why they adopted you into their genetic line in the first place. It is what makes you worthy of the Lord Jesus' divine heritage.

Exemplifying Your Heavenly Heritage

God intended human worship forms to exemplify and extend His heavenly culture to our clay world once He engrafted Himself in our clay bodies. He replenished this planet for the express purpose of reproducing Himself in His final species, humanity. Your communion, fellowship, worship, and service all mean to reenact for you and the world, the excellence of your divine nativity. Do not be deceived. Despite the suppression and dismissal of the new birth's doctrine, over the last several decades or so, Christianity is still exclusively about the Godhead's genetics disseminated by Jesus Christ. It alone makes a Christian and becoming a Christian is your only way back home to His world. Everything outside of these two objectives simply images the new life force deposited within you and demonstrates its power over your Adamic lineage.

As you grow in the Lord, that life force gradually transforms you into the Godhead's life form. The scripture passages, referred to earlier, show Jesus saying it best, "I am from above"; "you are from beneath". "I am not of this world" and because of it, you who are mine "are not of this world" either. Using many like statements, the Savior reveals His true identity and nativity as being from outside of earth. In numerously veiled and candid ways, our Lord discloses in the Gospels and later through His apostles in the epistles, the uniqueness that sets Him above those He came to save, and consequently what makes His faith supreme to that of the fallen gods He incarnated to dethrone. **Learning Task:** Do the following as a group before you find out about how to secure Jesus' divine heritage.

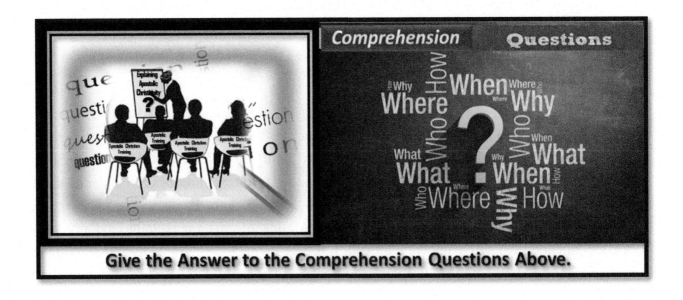

Give the Answer to the Comprehension Questions Above.

Sharing Jesus' Divine Heritage

John chapter 3 records the Savior instructing His future siblings and subjects on how they will partake of His divine heritage. They will be born (again) of God from above, not according to human reproductive processes but according to the very ones that brought Jesus into existence. Where is above? Above is heaven, the Messiah's real homeland and the birthplace of creation's first civilization. Proverbs 8 calls it the world that preceded the "primordial dust of the earth", according to the KJV.

Heaven's indomitable civilization was well developed by the time Creator God began His later creative works, such as the creation of the earth and our world. That world serves as the archetype governing all else that the Maker brings into existence. Besides us Christians, that world is the only thing that predates His every creative work. Since we were in Christ before the world began, we predate every other thing the Maker created and produced.

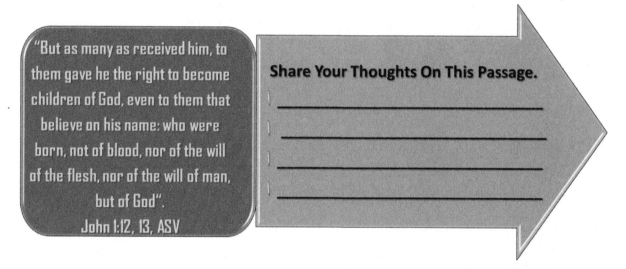

"But as many as received him, to them gave he the right to become children of God, even to them that believe on his name: who were born, not of blood, nor of the will of the flesh, nor of the will of man, but of God".
John 1:12, 13, ASV

Share Your Thoughts On This Passage.

In the sense described above, Christianity qualifies as the world and creation's first civilization, because it precedes sin, death, earth, and hell. No other faith can honestly make that claim. Christianity did not only need this world to be born, but also to be born again. This fact puts Genesis' "let us make man in our image and according to our likeness" in a different light. It adds purpose and clarity to God's reasons for making us on earth.

Activity: Answer the following and discuss as a study group:

1. What is to be learned from what you have read so far?
2. How do these revelations affect your faith, worship, and devotion to God?
3. What should every Christian get from this teaching?

Disciple Your Apostolic Christians With Training Games

Come Up with Fun Ways to Build Confidence And Competence

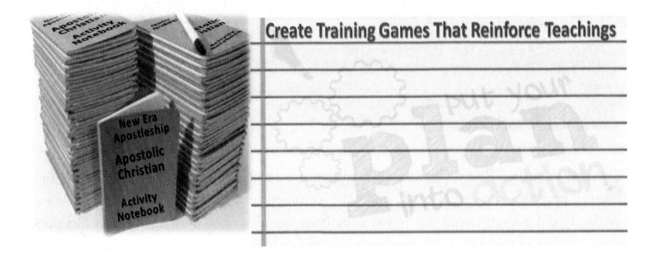

Create Training Games That Reinforce Teachings

New Era Apostleship

Apostolic Christian

Activity Notebook

Reading Review

1. Springing from the Godhead's family tree is Christianity's mystery.
2. Church forms and worship are to attract others to be saved and show our gratitude.
3. All Christians are to demonstrate God's powerful age to come.
4. Christians owe God and Christ for paying the ransom for their souls, they owe them their life and loyalty.

UNIT 8

How Christianity Became the Almighty's First Civilization

God begot Jesus Christ first and then put us in Him before making anything else. It is why and how Jesus holds the title of "first begotten". His Father deposited us in His first begotten Son the way our offspring and their generations reside in human bodies as sperm and eggs. Jesus' spiritual sperm is what begets us again to God and what makes the Godhead our parent. Peter says it this way:

"Being born again, not of corruptible seed, but of incorruptible, by the word of God, which liveth and abideth forever". 1 Peter 1:23

Being born again by God's Word and will is how we become eternal citizens, temporarily stationed in this world. The new birth makes us citizens of creation's oldest civilization, the supernal kingdom of the Most High God. Becoming a Spirit-filled Christian gives us our "born from above" status and entitles us, as earth-born seeds, to abide in Creator God's secluded, celestial paradise when we depart this world. Insight of this nature is vital to your Christian faith because it influences how you behave in Him, and it shapes the habits you take into eternity. The strength of your faith and fidelity to God lies in understanding

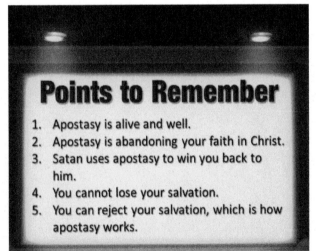

Points to Remember

1. Apostasy is alive and well.
2. Apostasy is abandoning your faith in Christ.
3. Satan uses apostasy to win you back to him.
4. You cannot lose your salvation.
5. You can reject your salvation, which is how apostasy works.

how you became a Christian and appreciating why you want to remain one. Together, these details reinforce why your salvation is worth fighting for and worth defending.

Fight for Your Salvation—Endure to the End

Today Satan's hostile machine works relentlessly to overthrow Jesus Christ's redemption of you. Daily, it mercilessly pummels your faith in Him with the goal of reversing what the Messiah did on the cross and its effects in your being. That machine aims to recover the Lord's converts who once served many gods (and any god), who are now serving His Father as the true and living God. In the subtlest ways they carry out their schemes to draw you <u>away</u> from Him. There is a word for this tactic. It is the word *apostasy*. In fact, the basic meaning of the word <u>apostasy</u> is "to draw one away from his or her faith".

In the Christian's case, apostasy means, *"to draw one of God's children away from Him, their eternal Father, to return the convert to the natural father's doomed gods"*. Restoring your soul to the service of your human family's generation gods is underlying goal of apostasy. It seeks to nullify your obligations to Jesus Christ so you can go back to being who you were before Him. Sadly, and recklessly, the word <u>apostasy</u> and all of its dangers has all but been eliminated from modern Christian doctrine. Yet, it was seen as a real threat by the early apostles. They wrestled constantly with the spirits of people's old lives because they recognized that saying the sinner's prayer, so to speak, was just the beginning of their walk with the Lord. The apostles defended their young converts from their old spirits because they knew it would be some time before they could detect the enemies of their soul, let alone defend themselves from them. They also knew the Lord to be loving and severe, jealous and merciful, and holy and righteous. These traits of God's character long ago predetermined His stance on humanity, His family, and His response to earthly sin. Whether in or out of His Son's redemption, the Lord anticipated and resolved humanity's reactions to His righteousness before ever uttering "Let there Be…".

All of the Almighty's earthly and afterlife decisions and judgments were settled long before Genesis 1:26, 27, which is why His pronouncements on sin are irrevocable. God is holy and He prizes His holiness above everything. It is just only because He cannot change that He is holy, but it is also because He does not want to change. The Lord's unalterableness means He can never reverse Himself in the future on what He decreed and condemned in the past. The way His unchanging nature affects your salvation is this: While no one can reverse your new birth's spiritual genetics, some things can seduce you into so profaning your new spirit that the damage done to it is irreparable: This is what John the Apostle means when he says there is sin leading to a death that no prayers can avert. See 1 John 5:16. Apostasy is one sin that leads to death. It ends in death because there is no alternative or solution to renouncing Jesus Christ and rejecting His salvation. As the last sacrificial offering heaven has to give for human sin, renouncing Him and defecting from Him leaves God with no other means of redeeming you.

It is now time to process this information. Guided by the chart below, give some thought to what persuaded or failed to persuade you the most about Apostolic Christianity, based on what you just read. Use the template below to model how you will present your thoughts and reactions on this material to others. If you were not persuaded, jot down what you need to know, learn, and master to become convinced that Apostolic Christians are a genuine necessity. If you are persuaded, fill in the same information to share with others. Outline what they and you need to know to learn and to master to become effective disciplers of Apostolic Christians. When you are done, go on to learn more about apostasy.

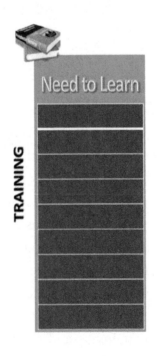

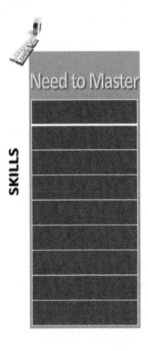

Avoid Apostasy

The fallen spirits manipulating your vulnerability to apostasy want you back. They want your salvation nullified and your New Creation life neutralized so the Lord will evict you from His celestial populations forever. They know when that happens you will leave earth failing to qualify to reenter Christ your Savior's world, and so be doomed to hell under their rule. Remember this, sin may manifest as an impulse, but in reality its seduction is a well calculated stratagem that serves way beyond your satisfaction. The game plan is to get you to apostatize because apostasy nullifies the New Creation and cancels your eternal citizenship. It also deteriorates the process that made you like Jesus Christ and makes you too corrupt for God's celestial world.

Yes, it is true as just stated; you cannot lose your salvation, meaning some invisible force cannot snatch it out of you. However, it is a gift that the Lord put in your possession, and so, yours to protect. What many Christian teachers and leaders today do not affirm is that your salvation is also yours to reject. Converts reject Jesus Christ all the time. Just reading His words about "enduring to the end" tells you that He expects it. Like many others, you too can tell God you tried it, did not like it, and refuse to do what it takes to maintain it. People leave the Lord every second of every day, some of them on purpose and others without knowing what they are doing. The Lord's Parable of the Seed, the Sower, and the Word in the Gospels make this very plain. As do Matthew 7:21-23.

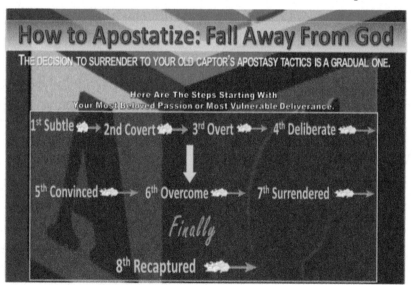

Not everyone that says the sinner's prayer is committed to living it out to the end, especially when the proving process that sifts who deserves eternal life from who does not heats up. The trials of redemption life have a twofold purpose. They are designed to separate the true from the false and to strengthen our mortal souls for immortal living. Over the ages, heaven's rigorous tests have disqualified many who started out pursuing Jesus who could not endure to the end.

Recorded in Matthew 13:18 and Mark 4:14, the three versions of the parable show that Jesus has quick starters and fast finishers. He has the "try hard" until it hurters and "the endure" to the enders. Still there is something you <u>must</u> know about the Lord and His afterlife. God's world is called heaven because it is a place, not a belief system. You should know that when you leave this body, you are not relocating to a cluster of clouds or stars, but to a real planet, with real citizens, under a long-standing government. Christians are saved to be redeemed after death by a <u>person</u> not an experience. That person will transport them to a realm, not a religion.

In God's world, that has been around since what we call forever, there is no great steeple-clad-edifice or a library of religious alternatives waiting to serve you when you arrive. There will be no buffet of spiritual preferences or idealized philosophies for you to accept or reject. Heaven is where Jesus Christ, the judge of the quick and the dead, rules and reigns uncontested. In God's world, there is no other ruler and its citizens want it to stay that way. They do not want another God ruling them, nor are they wishing their Maker were not what He is. His world's creatures are not hoping to change their God. They live utterly in love with Him. The perpetual residents of His kingdom are quite content with the Almighty's ways and laws, and happily celebrate Him with ceaseless adoration. Likewise, Jesus is the only King they want; they are not seeking to replace Him. Not one of those populating His eternal spheres desires to replace any member of the Godhead. The one and only creature that did want to usurp them was cast out and is now earth's problem and no longer theirs.

When Jesus as the Messiah wraps up this age, saved souls are neither going to a huge never-ending church service, nor are they entering an everlasting resort with options for migrating in and out of hell, should heaven get too boring, or hell get too hot. Heaven and hell are not equal territories that one only needs a passport to travel back and forth between them to have the best of both worlds. Also, hell has no transit system that whisks you to heaven for a visit or vice versa, and it has no paroles or reprieves. They are two eternal extremes with one-way entrances and no way out. The absoluteness of both jurisdictions say why Jesus had to become a sin-ridden human to get into hell. Taking on sin was the only way the crucified Son of God could qualify to enter the realm of the doomed and dead to retrieve the souls He incarnated to save. To get out of hell, our Savior had to be justified[35] by His Father, which was the only way He could return to heaven with the souls He redeemed. Answer the following questions before

---

[35] Vindicated, made acceptable, corrected, warranted, validated, excused, aligned, adjusted, straightened, aligned: To prove or show to be just, right, or reasonable.

reading what heaven is really like. **Answer** the for a group discussion that explores deeper your expectations of your faith as compared to that of the Lord's early church.

1) What is heaven?

2) What is heaven not?

3) How do you convince people heaven is real?

4) What kind of people would not want to go to heaven, and why?

What Heaven Is Really Like?

Those who make it into God's world will not "just walk around heaven all day". They will join Him in His eternity-to-eternity lifestyle and work, taking their place as leaders and taking up their duties as laborers to expand and sustain all of His realms. Heaven's preexistence makes the contest for your immortal soul real because the prize is your permanent citizenship in one world or the other. Your eternal obligation to the ruler of the light or the darkness is a choice only you alone can make. Once you make it in this world, that decision is final and the Lord will honor throughout all eternity. Do not be misled; the consequences of that decision are completely out of your control. Whatever the Lord says both worlds hold for its residents (past, present and future) is what you will live with forever.

The Almighty is who He says He is, and as the Maker of all things, He has the supreme right to demand what He wants in His world. That right extends to having things the way He wants them. The Lord also has the incontestable prerogative to make the rules for His realm and to enforce them as He sees fit. He alone as Creator possesses the ageless wisdom to govern the creatures He made and has the absolute authority to accept or reject each one based on His own criteria. The rights that humans flaunt at God so arrogantly, literally began with Him and not with them. Nature's unpreventable devastations and life's inevitable everyday tragedies affirm these realities. Besides all this, Creator God is the ancient of days. He and His societies have lasted a long time. As such, their world long ago worked through the issues that our world still grapples with today. God's eternality and His world's longevity indicate they resolved, eons ago, the destructive powers that threaten our existence. For example, take crime: Matthew 6:20 answers it with Jesus revealing that in heaven there is no crime. They also have no decay (rust), decadence, burglaries, or thefts. Since people cannot die there is evidence that there are no murders, slaughters, or terminal illnesses are in God's world either. Prophetic writings imply they had them at one time, but they dealt with their culprits and causes and restored their world. Consequently, heaven's historical clashes with celestial sin and sinners make our joining them in their world in our fallen state not only too risky, but also impossible.

Shed Some Light

Then entrance of they word gives light; it gives understanding to the simple.
Psalm 119:130

Jot Down Some Points of Enlightenment On What Was Just Discussed

_____

_____

_____

_____

_____

The Almighty's Way is the Only Way

To have everything His way, the Most High exerted strenuous effort - at great cost -to structure His world the way He wants it to be forever. His highest objective was to assure it remained impermeable to sin and, completely indomitable in the future, no matter how powerful the creatures to come from Him were made. Foreseeing events that could require Him to have to restore His kingdom, God devised perceptive devices to weed out any threat or defect that could crop up in His creation: proactively at first and then later protectively, should the inevitable happen, which it did. He put impermeable counter measures in place, and within His citizens to eliminate any likelihood of recurring catastrophes or revolutions. Shrewd systems were installed to reinforce His world with even tighter controls and restraints than those that exposed the iniquity in the heart of the anointed cherub that sought to seize it. During its restoration when the inevitable happened, He moved to preclude[36] any hint of invasion or uprising in the future. Inviolable[37] laws and a creation-wide justice system see to it. Therefore, the laws and rules we scoff at here on earth are actually the safety measures He put in place to guard His eternal realms. Before hell broke loose in heaven, earth's despised laws served as His contingencies; they still do. After the unprecedented crisis was contained, they became His precautions. Once the Lord got things the way He desired, He encoded creation with deterrents that watch over everything He restored to make His world forever impregnable.

---

[36] To rule out in advance. To make impossible, especially beforehand.
[37] Unbreakable, firm, sacred, holy, untouchable, sanctified, immune, incontaminate, imperviable.

Expending a great deal of time and energy, the Most High built His world to self-perpetuate His way. The self-perpetuation, however, rested as much on the citizens to populate it as much as it relied on His inscrutable[38] protections to safeguard them. From the inside out, each creature in the Maker's realm was renovated and its citizens regenerated to guarantee that all recipients of His eternal life possessed the capacity and integrity to coexist in our Lord's restricted domains. Everything that is to reside with Him must be completely compatible with

Him to gain access. God's main compatibility requirement is one hundred percent conformance to His creation and total agreement with His vision for it.

Only those rejoicing in His reign are welcome to reside and rule with Him forever. Disagreers and revolters are immediately banished to avert a repeat of the rebellions that marred His original civilization. The actions, initiatives, and decisions regarding who will be heaven or

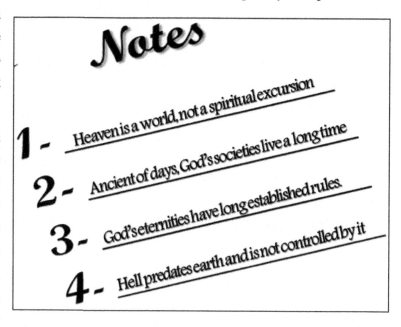

Notes

1- Heaven is a world, not a spiritual excursion

2- Ancient of days, God's societies live a long time

3- God's eternities have long established rules.

4- Hell predates earth and is not controlled by it

who is hell bound were predetermined in God's timeless age. They are not something He came up with and imposed after He created earth, replenished it, or His reactions to Adam's fall. The Godhead's swift response to that catastrophe implies that He was prepared in advance for that eventuality. To stay ahead of "come what may", the Lord ensured that everything He did and desired was well constituted by the time His human species and its generations began.

As you can see, history and experience (more than religious rigidity) motivate the Lord's criteria for the type of souls He will bless with His eternal life. Nothing His later creatures demand can overturn what He instituted in His world before our times. Eternal punishments and rewards began in the spirit realms, not in this physical one, making the place of ultimate punishment a province of God's spiritual jurisdiction, not earth's. Hell, the prison for eternal criminals predates humanity because in the beginning it was created to incarcerate spirits and souls, not flesh and bones. Hell came forth as eternal not temporal. Its first function was to confine the immortal world's criminals, which means it exclusively complies with eternity's unending governments. Human ordinances have no effects on the afterlife whatsoever.

---

[38] Impenetrable, mysterious, indecipherable.

Hell, like death and the grave, is of spiritual origin. So affecting or amending its codes and regulations is way beyond mortals' capability and authority. Like everything else beyond the world of flesh and blood, hell has no physical properties and makes no provision for human tampering. To prove these realities for the earthbound, life itself reminds us that death obligates us to God's sovereign will every single day. Its absoluteness does not respond to anything humans can do. When it is sent to collect what God wants to remove from the planet, it is unapologetic. Death never explains itself; it does not ask permission, and it will not sympathize with the sorrow it causes. Death never repents or regrets, nor does it excuse itself; it just does its job. These realisms underlie the ways the afterlife is strictly on God's sovereign terms, and is not subject to mankind's whims, imaginations, or presumption.

Eternal Life is on God's Terms

To wrap this up, over the eons it took for Him to get life in His world the way He desires it, God gave great thought and took intractable precautions to defend His kingdom, and all those inhabiting it at the time. If that was His only response, what He achieved would be remarkable enough, but that is not all He did. Realizing that His creative works were far from over, the Lord appended to His then present systems, exhaustive safeguards to secure His future species, and extended those safeguards to His other worlds. So the recovery and safekeeping works the Lord's restorations imposed came down from Him as heaven-to-earth rules that reached beyond His current civilizations, all the way into the future. Meticulous restitutions and enhancements were made to all that survived the incursions that put creation at risk to assure that whatever enjoyed His endlessness forever conformed to His minutest whim. In the process, while waiting for you and me to be saved and to join Him there, the Almighty endured (and continues to endure) much long suffering to keep His word and to fulfill His promises.

Flesh out with your study group how what you just learned can be walked out in the modern Christian's life. Consider today's temptations, culture, and lax Christianity.

Draw up a list of what you have envisioned to be the identifiers of your Apostolic Christianity conversion.

From what has been said so far, you now have ample reason to dispute anyone that tries to convince you that your God will swing wide the doors of heaven in the end and let every and anybody into it. Our God will not unleash on His worlds those He judged, condemned, and even destroyed in hell before you and I were born. If that were His intent, He would not have kept Adam and his wife out of the Garden of Eden after they became inhabited by the spirit hiding in the serpent.

Practically speaking, it would not be prudent for God to empty out hell into heaven, or to reward what hates Him on earth with eternal life. There is just no payoff for Him to do so. If He were so foolish as to inflict upon Himself and His populations the very villains He quarantined for ages for their corruption, it would make Him quite irresponsible, to say the least. Doing so would forever enslave the Most High and His kingdom to the horrors, anguish, and abuses they have endured for ages. Besides that, His agony over sin would be incessant.

No, the single motivation for God's longsuffering is not to lose one soul ordained to His Son's salvation. If He reversed Himself on this matter, there would be no way for Him to rid Himself of the billions of evildoers who would possess His eternal life. With hell no longer being an option, He would have no remedy for wickedness. Finally, eliminating hell as His prison means God would get no relief from sin's sorrows and have no hope of ever enjoying peace and tranquility again.

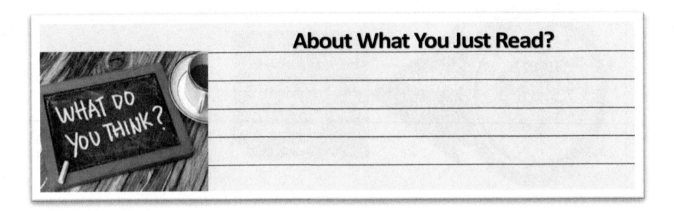

About What You Just Read?

You see, God's longsuffering with humanity ensures nothing worthy of Him and His salvation is lost. His tolerance was never meant to eternalize the human atrocities He endures today. It was to separate His Son's wheat from the Devil's tares. To subject Himself and those who conformed to His righteousness to endless calamity in place of the peace and prosperity He now enjoys just makes no sense. To put it bluntly, human sin and perversion have well proven their effects. What spirits and souls will do outside of mortal flesh is no guessing game to heaven. God knows from experience what to expect from the beings He brought into existence. He harbors no delusions about what comes out of the exercise of their free will. The Lord knows all this because He has seen it, lived it, and fought it all before. Having long ago evicted sin and its devastation from His world, He has no incentive to revisit those eras, or to expose His recuperated citizenry to it again.

The mushy love peddled by some preachers and teachers of this age has no place in God's wisdom because it is detrimental to His self-preservation. He is adamant about not accommodating any such opposition or destruction again. Holding all the cards and controlling all souls underpins His resolve, not to mention that there is just nothing in it for the Lord. In human terms, God has no upside to softening His stance on the sin and the rebellion He has already condemned and restrains. The idea of His relaxing the righteousness standards that have guarded His kingdom so far is ludicrous, and indulging it offers Him and guarantees Him nothing but endless sorrow. Read Revelation 21:27 to make some biblical connections between what it says and what you just learned about God's afterlife attitude toward humanity.

What It Says & Means To Me

1)

2)

3)

4)

5)

To continue our previous discussion, besides all that has been said so far, you should know that when the Almighty's ideal world did come under attack, He spared no effort to restore it. Exhaustive labors accompanied exorbitant reparations to improve what He had before the cherub's revolution ruptured everything. In the process, those extreme (and irreversible) measures we talk about above were enacted to ensure that our God never has to tolerate incompatible or corruptible beings in eternity again. A fervent vow to not repeat heaven's turbulent history fell to Jesus Christ His Son to fulfill, something John 10:9 asserts. Jesus, the door to eternity will see that His Father never again has to endure what they lived when "iniquity was found in that cherub." That is what the Messiah is saying in John chapter 10 when He declares His guardianship over the Almighty's sheepfolds.

As the first begotten Son, the Savior cannot let anything get through to His Father's world that fails their naturalization and sanctification processes. After what they all went through, the Godhead finds it too unsafe to expose itself or its populations to satanic ambitions or resentments again. For them, it is all just that cut and dried, no matter how hard line it appears to those who did not suffer their sorrows. That is why they are not exporting earth's problems to heaven. Doing so would nullify the creation-wide cleansing of Jesus' blood as the supreme remedy for purging sin. In effect they would only be forced to wrestle with the tragic events that spread sin throughout creation in the first place all over again. The Godhead's resoluteness on this matter can be discerned from its words in Genesis 3:22. In an all too familiar sounding anticipatory tone, they respond to Adam's transgression with the following words. Refreshing yourself on them prepares you for our revisit to the Garden of Eden.

> *"And the LORD God said, Behold, the man is become as one of us, to know good and evil: and now, lest he put forth his hand, and take also of the tree of life, and eat, and live forever:"*

Revisiting the Garden of Eden

What revisiting Eden wants you to perceive about the Godhead is this. What happened to Adam and his wife, was caused by the very creature that destabilized eternity before this world was. His rebellion changed all the rules for heaven and its realms. Remembering the spiritual repercussions of Satan's heavenly uprising, and how it spread, made containing the cascading damages the first couple ignited a number one imperative. The implications of the man's disobedience and the motives of the spirit behind it, made allowing the couple to return to the Garden of Eden to eat its eternal life fruit a deadly indulgence. As yet, the Devil had not put the idea in Adam's mind, but it was only a matter of time before he would to capitalize off his earlier success. This time he was sure to meet with much less resistance. Perhaps once more, he could use the woman to seduce her man.

Build a Profile of What You Just Read Looks Like

Putting the Pieces Together

_____

_____

_____

_____

_____

_____

To get phase two of his plan underway, the adversary could urge the doomed couple to save themselves by eating from the tree of life. Maybe this time he could imply they would go back to before all hell broke loose within and around them if they did. If he could get them to eat from the tree of life, Adam's now demonic virility would give the Devil re-access to heaven. By using Adam's seed to reproduce himself in the woman, he could spawn his seed throughout eternity relying on Adam's image and likeness to the Godhead to enable it. The prospects of which would be infinitely catastrophic for the Almighty.

As you can see from the referred to text, even voicing the fallout from the Devil's plan aloud was unthinkable to the Lord. So, He forever banished the couple to protect Himself and His world, and to preserve the future He had planned for both. Complete the next couple of exercises below and then read "Barring the Way to the Tree of Life".

M.I.N.D. the Word Activity

"For who hath known the mind of the Lord, that he may instruct him? But we have the mind of Christ." 2 Corinthians 2:16

The M.I.N.D. the Word Activity seeks to guide your personal use of the scriptures in your daily life. It gives you the opportunity to fuse the passage's wisdom with your soul and then allow it to instruct you on the behaviors that you feel you need corrected to properly fulfill your duty to God's truth in action.

Scripture: Genesis 3:22

Motive: Why did God include it in His Bible?

Answer:

Instruction: What does God want to teach you from this passage?

Lesson:

You have just been given a large amount of insight into the pre-earth world and the precarnate life of the Godhead that necessitated its second member to take on flesh and enter the planet. What should have stood out to you most of all is God's side of the story. For ages we have heard the salvation gospel focus exclusively on humanity with little to no attention given to what preceded it, or caused its ruin. The explanations you just read gave you the backstory on how Adam's transgression affected the Lord and His entire creation. It answers why Ephesians 1:10 reads the way it does. Ask yourself, why did God have to include heavenly things in Christ's supposed earthly salvation. When and how were they affected? The answer to that question should be intriguing. Spend time with your study group discussing it a bit to see what everyone concludes from the through exchanges.

Activity: With the answers to the previous activities in mind, engage in the following activity with your training group to practice focusing your answers on the value of Apostolic Christianity in today's world, how best to go about it. Outline what it will take to convince others, especially traditionalists to do the same.

Apostolic Christian

FOCUS GROUP

DISCUSSION TOPIC
Talk out ways to expand the ways an evangelical thinker's mind to grasp and respect God's sovereign side as an Apostolic Christian does.

Barring the Way to the Tree of Life

You see, in their fallen state and utterly possessed by Satan inhabiting the serpent, the doomed first couple could be used to re-spread Satan's doom and chaos to all heaven's deathless creatures. That is something the Lord could never allow. After all, controlling what the gullible couple had already done on earth would be difficult enough. Reversing the spread of their devilish seed throughout eternity would be nearly impossible. Particularly, since humans began life more like His Firstborn Son than His angels did. So wisdom, and experience, dictated that keeping Adam out of the garden and away from the tree of life was a prudent response to their tragedy on the part of the Godhead. With the preservation of all those that populated heaven's first civilization being at stake, past and present, the Creator was the only person capable of remedying it. Everyone else was under its burden. Thus, Creation's Maker alone had the power and knowhow to reverse demonic crises. The experience gained from overturning it in heaven made curtailing the destruction Adam's sin spawned not too difficult. On earth, His first step to doing so began with barring their access to the tree of life.

Action: Answer the following questions and share your response with your study group:

1)	What is apostasy?
2)	Why did God create hell?
3)	Why can God not let everybody into heaven?
4)	Why could the man and woman not be trusted to remain in the garden?
5)	Why is God so picky about who can enter heaven?
6)	What should a person do to guarantee access to God's world?

You Control Your Soul

The preceding explanations and examples give you some idea of how serious your Christianity is and how deadly apostasy is to it. You now know what God really thinks about those who surrender their sinless, saved soul to His enemy. Adam was pure, just like you are in Christ. The cherub that desecrated heaven was likewise sinless. He was sinless until, as Isaiah says, "iniquity was found in" him. However, when Adam became God's adversary by obeying the Devil that tempted him, his apostasy cost him his place in God's world forever, the way the Devil's anarchy cost him his eternal home. It was not just the disobedience that doomed Adam. It was also the spiritual and physical effects of that disobedience as well. So bear these truths in mind when you assume nothing can cost you your eternal destiny. Your soul's condition can and will risk it because salvation depends on holiness, without which no one can see the Lord. You see, redemption holiness relies on your compliance with the Lord's Spirit of life from Christ Jesus that was deposited in you. It alone has the power to keep you pure enough to enter and abide in God's world forever. Your hope and intents, however sincere, are not enough.

Soul condition determines who will spend eternity where, not the good deeds that are applauded by this world. Many people are good enough for this world and while they are alive, it will reward them for their goodness. However, only one type of creature is conducive to God's world, the replicas of the Lord Jesus Christ who carry the seal of His reproduction. That seal, is the indwelling Holy Spirit who purifies the spirit and soul from all sin.

Below, share your thoughts on what you just read. Afterward, enlarge your appreciation of your salvation by learning what it takes to secure it.

About What You Just Read?

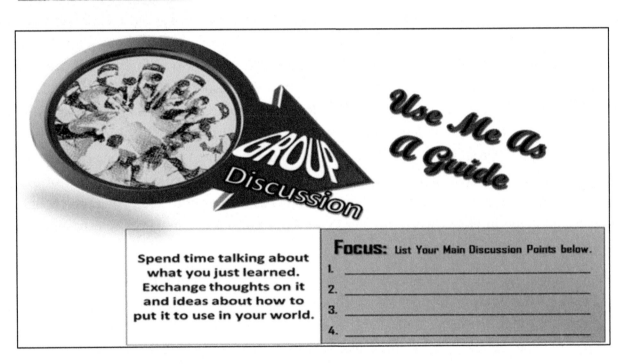

Spend time talking about what you just learned. Exchange thoughts on it and ideas about how to put it to use in your world.

Focus: List Your Main Discussion Points below.

1. _____
2. _____
3. _____
4. _____

Secure Your Salvation

What all you have been reading so far means is this: Even though your salvation made you just like Jesus, His faith too was tested. His Father put the sin of the world on Him and when He did, it disqualified Him from returning to His heavenly home. If being laden with the sin of this world sent the innocent Son of God to hell, how much more will His Father sentence those who commit sins (worthy of death) to go there?[39] Not a lot of Christians know that Jesus went to hell. Not knowing this truth leads them to believe they can do whatever they want with their New Creation spirit and still escape it. That is a mistake that reading Psalm 16:10, Acts 2:27 explain.

While it is quite comforting to hear the minister say that God forgives and forgets all, there are a couple of things you should consider before accepting their words at face value. What you are about to read just may make you rethink your faith in them, since unfounded opinions could cost you eternal life.

In comparing what your favorite minister says about God, heaven, and hell to what is written in scripture, be guided by the Lord Jesus' words in Matthew chapter 5. He asserts that the kind of "carte blanche" salvation theology, so popular today, does not totally wash when it is contrasted with His word.

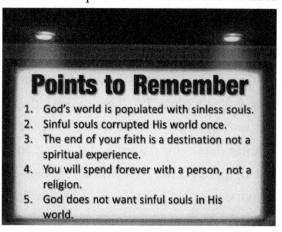

Points to Remember
1. God's world is populated with sinless souls.
2. Sinful souls corrupted His world once.
3. The end of your faith is a destination not a spiritual experience.
4. You will spend forever with a person, not a religion.
5. God does not want sinful souls in His world.

For example, ask yourself if God forgets all, then why does He keep a record of people's lives in books to open for His end of the world judgments. Think about it. What is the point of promising rewards and condemnations if it will not matter in the end? Jesus Himself said in John 5:29 that in the resurrection those that have done good rise from death to life and those that have done evil rise from their graves to the lake of fire. His words suggest that it is shortsighted to teach a resurrection that only rewards good when scripture bluntly says all will rise, each one to his or her earned everlasting recompense. Clearly, there is an accounting to be made to the Judge of the quick and the dead, that every soul born on earth must give. That accounting is the reason for the phrase "Judgment Day".

---

[39] See Hebrews 10:29.

Read Related Scripture Hebrews 10:29; Psalm 16:10; Acts 2:27

Up Close Study

Discuss What You Just Read and Depict Your Thoughts Using Word Pictures

God's Righteousness is Nonnegotiable

Romans 14:17 and Ephesians 5:10 have several things in common. The two that stand out the most are the Holy Spirit and God's righteousness. Not changing from the Exodus to the New Testament, God declares that He is holy and those to be with Him forever, must be holy as He is holy. Holiness is the essence and context of heaven. It is the substance of its citizens and the climate of their world. That holiness includes a nonnegotiable righteousness that God defines, not our culture, its courts, or our times. If you happen to be one of those who mistake mercy for grace and our God's imputed righteousness for unchecked Christian liberty, you should read 2 Corinthians 7:1. There it says that your spirit and flesh can be made filthy. That filth if left uncleansed will deteriorate your New Creation spirit the way rebellion and unbelief cost Lucifer his divine nature and his heavenly home, and also the way Adam's disbelief cast him out of his pristine habitation. Take a lesson from these two events. See that you do not convince yourself that God will not send you to hell because He loves you too much. Besides the Lord hating sin and not wanting it in His presence ever again, you should know that He loved Jesus long before He saved you. Yet He still sent Jesus to hell for the sin that He Himself put upon Him. Imagine the holiness of God being so inviolable that even His first begotten Son, Co-Creator, and Sovereign of creation could not get back into His heavenly birthplace sin ridden. That is what John's Gospel records Jesus addressing, see 17:5. Cross-reference it with Acts 2:27.

So, on the question of who goes to heaven and who goes to hell, the real issue is not will God send the sin ridden to hell; He has already proved that He will and has to do so. The better question is how it will disqualify you to get back into heaven where your spirit-self began. And, are you willing to do whatever it takes to return there? The answer to both questions may expose you to a different side of yourself that reveals a different story altogether.

Next, we talk about Christianity being a nationality and not just another religion. If you see being one as something more than faith in your heart, what is to come will make perfect sense to you. After reading it, you will certainly find yourself able to discern the signs of your Apostolic Christianity. Before that though, complete the following exercises.

Activity: Before reading on, complete the following exercise on Christianity as a nation. The information to come will enlighten you on the value of your new birth.

M.I.N.D. the Word Activity

"For who hath known the mind of the Lord, that he may instruct him? But we have the mind of Christ." 2 Corinthians 2:16

The M.I.N.D. the Word Activity seeks to guide your personal use of the scriptures in your daily life. It gives you the opportunity to fuse the passage's wisdom with your soul and then allow it to instruct you on the behaviors that you feel you need corrected to properly fulfill your duty to God's truth in action.

Scripture: Hebrews 10:29; Psalm 16:10; Acts 2:27; 2 Corinthians 7:1

Motive: Why did God include it in His Bible?

Answer:

Instruction: What does God want to teach you from this passage?

Lesson:

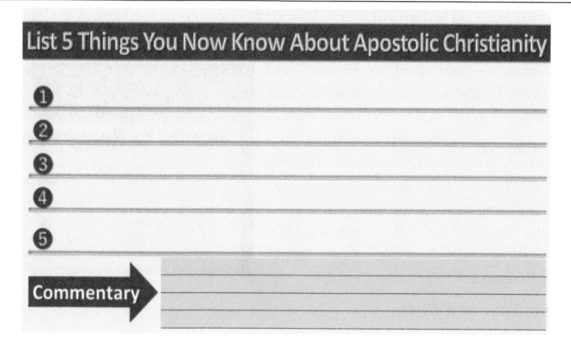

List 5 Things You Now Know About Apostolic Christianity

1.
2.
3.
4.
5.

Commentary

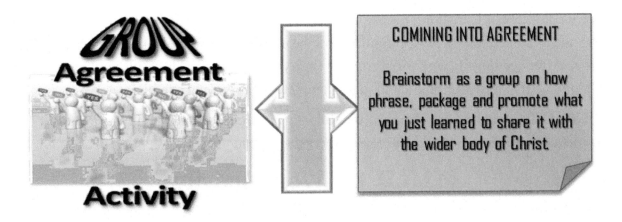

Really a Nation, Not Just a Religion

In God and Christ's mind, the Christian church on earth is the literal <u>nation</u> of Jesus Christ. This is so because the ecclesia was begotten by a King, a heavenly King. The church of the Lord Jesus Christ comes directly from the Godhead's divine nature. As a result, being born again by Christ Jesus, the King of kings, did two things for you and me: First, it reproduced us as God's offspring; second, it transferred us from Adam's genealogy to Christ's lineage. The two together made us royal immortals. When those two things happened, we who are saved lost our exclusive classification as citizens of this world, spiritually speaking. In resuming our eternal nationality, which is that of the living and true God and His Christ, our spirits' transcended this world and its citizenry to rejoin the family of God in heaven. That is one of the many reasons scripture declares we are in heavenly places in Christ Jesus. Only this time, we return there in full human divine form. Imagine the ingenuity and technology the Lord used to make that happen.

The moment we were saved, we restarted (and reset) our heavenly existence. Nothing less than that could give us the right to resume our original divine state, except that we resided in Jesus Christ's body in the heavens, long before anything else began. Being born of the God and Father of Jesus Christ verifies that you are theirs. It does not just <u>make</u> you one of theirs; it in reality <u>manifests</u> you as one of theirs. You can confirm this by reading Romans 8:9.

Points to Remember

1. Our renewed spirits and transforming souls must be trained to master how Christ lives life.
2. Jesus' inheritance is now ours too.
3. The Lord left earth to prepare for the trillions of lives that will believe in Him and enter His world.

Valuing Your New Birth

The new birth notifies you and all creation that everything needed to secure your eternal destination was done before the foundation of the world. All that is required to ensure your eternal life when your spirit and soul depart this world was done in, and by Jesus Christ. Now getting there is largely up to you. You must learn to pray, to believe beyond the hurts, and to endure the hard stages of your Christian growth. You must fully surrender to God in order to resist the Devil that so wants you back. The good news is that even though it is on you to live out your salvation, God did not leave you to your own devices to keep it. He gave you His Holy Spirit and His Holy Word to help. Stay in both and you will do well.

Activity: After hearing about how and why hell exists, you should be more motivated to fight the good fight and fiercely guard your new birth. Answer the following and discuss as your responses a study group.

1. What makes Christianity more of a nation and less of a religion?
2. How do Christians lose their salvation?
3. Why is it, sometimes a fight to stay saved?
4. What does the new birth accomplish?
5. What does the new birth say to all worlds about you?
6. Say why God cannot let the sin ridden in hell.
7. Make several modern day connections between God's holiness and His righteous.

Why Hell Exists

Righteousness, sin, and death are the main reasons hell exists. Deuteronomy 32:22 alludes to another one. Go there to see if you can discover it. Meanwhile, to continue our discussion, sin and death (hell's most powerful agents), are what Jesus needed to take on to get into hell. Righteousness is what He needed to get out of it. That righteousness His Father pronounced upon Him when He justified His Son's sacrifice. God's judgment of righteousness is how Jesus broke the bonds of death to rise from the dead. To reiterate, if the sin-ridden Son of God deserved to go to hell as a Savior, how much more are those He delivered from the law of sin and death deserving of it for returning to their former life and its gods? God's justification reinserted us into Christ the way it got His Beloved Son out of hell. Declaring us as righteous as He is because we are His children, gives us the right to get back into heaven when our time on earth is done.

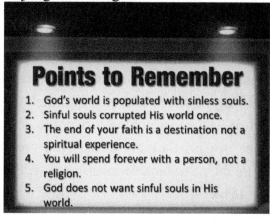

Points to Remember
1. God's world is populated with sinless souls.
2. Sinful souls corrupted His world once.
3. The end of your faith is a destination not a spiritual experience.
4. You will spend forever with a person, not a religion.
5. God does not want sinful souls in His world.

Our return to God's family is quite similar to the path Jesus took to get from heaven to earth. The difference is our spiritual journey passes us from death to life because of Christ's incorruptible seed within us. The Holy Spirit, in comparison, physically transported Jesus from heaven <u>to</u> earth as a seed and deposited Him in Mary's womb. The womb gave Him His human body and the ability to be killed. Our transition from death to life made us, spiritually speaking, just like the Godhead. Our eternal seed entered our mortal body the moment the Holy Spirit stepped into our beings. He arrested the agents of sin and death by superseding its laws with His Son's justification.

By the way, so that you can answer those who ask about Him, the Holy Spirit is the Almighty's and the Messiah's pervasive self. He is how the Godhead is everywhere present at the same time. The Holy Spirit is how God's offspring is assured of reentering their heavenly realms and living forever. Look at His relationship with Jesus Christ and God Almighty (your heavenly Father), from the statements made below.

I AM	The Spirit of God
I AM	The Spirit of Christ
I AM	The Spirit of your Father
I AM	The eternal Spirit

To Actually Life Forever

We as Christians only have to learn how to abandon the ways of this world and adopt Jesus' eternal life practices to prepare for the world that awaits us. Practicing Christianity is learning how Christ lives His life and imitating it. Doing so gets our souls ready to reside and thrive in His supernal world. In the meantime, as we adapt to our Savior's lifestyle, we get to spread a little of it on earth, while He transforms us into His image and likeness from the inside out. Everyone born from above by God's Holy Spirit must undergo this transformation. It is the key resource that trains our souls to live life as it is lived in the Messiah's world.

As we master Christ's way of life, the darkness in our souls gives way to Jesus' radiant and pure light. Going from glory to glory and faith to faith, increases the purity of that light in us until we become too bright for this world and must leave it to reenter His. That is the glory of God and Christ in us and why they are awaiting our fully matured entrance into their kingdom. All of heaven is looking forward to sharing the hope of Christ's glory in us. They are eager to share their inestimable inheritance with us when we arrive.

Everything that Jesus left behind in heaven to come to earth to redeem you and me is now part of our everlasting inheritance. His life breeds the glory that gathers and reserves our portion of His messianic birthright. The Messiah's wealth, majesty, wisdom, and power are all waiting for us to return home in full heavenly splendor, in order to partake of it. His incarnation, death, and resurrection were all to reinstall you into the Godhead's family tree, and to qualify you share their celestial opulence. Your worthiness to reap their extravagant existence began with Jesus destroying the works of the Devil and of the flesh. To accustom us to their way of life, our Savior implanted His divine nature in us to predispose us to work the works of God, the way Jesus did when He was on earth. And how He made us is not just as one of His handmade products, but as the Almighty's progeny[40], born of His very being.

Preparing Our New World for Us, Stocking Our New Souls for It

When Jesus said He was going to prepare a place for us, He was talking about preparing His world to receive His born again family from the earth. Envision heaven exploding with glorified inhabitants from this world as depicted in Revelation chapters 7, 14, 20:12, and 13. Eternity's boundless territories are to be increased by trillions of beings who are just like the Son of God Himself. His words in John 14:2, 3 reflect His awareness of what must happen (when the time comes[41]) to ready His world to receive and house the multitudes of beings from the earth. In effect, it has to be modified to assimilate a completely renovated Adamic-Messianic[42] species. What a magnificent picture. The struggles and perseverance we have on earth will earn us entry into the Lord's deathless civilization. Our reward is habitation in His trouble-free paradise that fulfills the ages-long desire Jesus voices in John 17:24, 25. *"Father, I will that where I am, they also whom thou hast given me may be with me: that they may see my glory which thou hast given me, because thou hast loved me before the creation of the world."* John 17:24. To resettle His new family in their eternal homeland, Jesus and His heavenly kingdom must make incalculable preparations for their arrival. Getting us ready to show up there takes more than any human mind can fathom, God or not, much is involved in bringing His massive family home. Our Redeemer however is well up to the task.

---

[40] From stem of progignere that means to "beget, descendants, offspring, lineage, race, family. Online Etymology Dictionary.
[41] John 14:2, 3.
[42] Jesus is called the Last Adam.

Group Discussion

Session

Focus _____

1. _____

2. _____

3. _____

4. _____

Spend time talking about what you just learned. Exchange thoughts on it and suggest some ideas about how to put it to use in your world.

Bringing the Family Home

The primary reason Jesus came to earth was to *beget* (not just get) God's long awaited family that was hid in Him. Bringing us home again to His Father was the Messiah's secret mission. Only this time He will present us not as seeds buried within Himself, but as fully formed everlasting human citizens of His kingdom. In Romans 8:19, Paul dubs this populace, the manifest sons (children) of God. To win our whole selves back to the Father, Christ had to show up on earth in the flesh "to save that which was lost". You might ask to whom we were lost. The answer is, we were lost to Jesus Christ and God His Father because Adam sold his descendants in exchange for deity status. Trillions of lives resided in Adam when he ate from the tree of the knowledge of good and evil. His rebellion killed the immaterial life of every seed God had deposited in him. Consequently, his seemingly insignificant transgression condemned his children's souls to hell. It took the cross, the grave, and the resurrection to reverse what he did. See Romans 5:12-16 and Matthew 18:11.

Through Calvary and the Lord Jesus' resurrection, God recovered Adam's lost generations. When Jesus redeemed their souls with His blood, it freed the Godhead to turn its attention to expanding their invisible realms to accommodate all those who come to God the Father through His Son. To fulfill their promise of eternal life, ethereal and literal preparations had to be made to receive the family soon to be resurrected and raptured from the earth. The entire ordeal will amount to a vast immigration when it happens.

Getting There from Here

The only way to immigrate the lost, now found family of God from earth to eternity, is in the Spirit of the Almighty's first begotten Son. When His innumerable New Creation population does get into God's world, it will need places to reside, work, worship, and rule. That is where those many mansions Jesus says are in His Father's house enter the picture. The Most High God's yearning for more children that are like Jesus is one of the things that moved Him to send His first begotten into this world. When you and I are occupying those magnificent edifices, His Father's yearning will see its fulfillment.

To make that possible, Jesus returned home with a monumental checklist of things to be done to ready His realm for our coming. His arrangements include expansion, renovations, institutions, and the magnification of their world to receive our coming. The Savior's main priority is to set up places throughout eternity for His throng of new siblings to thrive and reign with Him forever. So right now, with that goal in mind, the Lord Jesus is busily working to modify His eternal world to receive His first civilization's new species. On earth, He is enabling the souls He inhabits to qualify to make the trip. We can only imagine Him moving throughout His numberless universes to meet this demand. All we have to do is to get there to take our places as fully matured citizens of the world that created this one. After our welcome home

celebration, we will all get to work ruling and reigning with Him to fulfill our glorious destiny in Christ.

1. What did God the Father want from the very beginning?
2. Why was Matthew 18:11 used?
3. What is Jesus doing now?
4. What are 3 of the ways the Lord is preparing His world for our arrival?

Now here is the end of the matter. Once the Godhead concludes its shutdown of Adam and Satan's age of doomed mortals, and fulfills the number of "born from above" believers ordained to populate His new world to come, God's dreams will be realized. Then the real life of the Christian, reassembled with the first civilization above the clouds and stars, will begin.

The Source of This Training's Revelatory Information

All of this information comes from God's mysterious archives. It contains the narratives on how and why Christianity is not just another world religion, and what makes it not a religion at all. We journeyed to earth in Adam's seed, not unlike the Messiah did when He traveled from His heavenly abode in His Father's seed[43] to enter the earth. To get back home, He surrendered to unimaginable cruelty so as not to return to His world without His Father's beloved family. Jesus did what it took to give His Dad His heart's desire, which was recovery of all that was lost in Eden. Determined to accomplish His true mission, the Savior died on

---

[43] Read Galatians chapter 3.

earth to get into hell. If hell were not His destination, then His Father would have just brought Him back to heaven when He died on the cross. But hell was indeed the Messiah's ultimate destination. It is the reason He incarnated because hell is where God's doomed but deeply beloved family was condemned to go when it died. A number of them from Adam to Christ were already waiting there for His arrival to rescue them. **Activity**: Answer the following and discuss as a study group:

Final Activities to Tryout Your New Knowledge

SCRIPTURE R.E.M.I.N.D.E.R. EXERCISE

"Let this mind be in you, which was also in Christ Jesus…" Philippians 2:5

Scripture Study: **Revelation - Explanation - Mysteries - Insight - Need - Demonstration - Example - Relevance**

Put some thought into the scripture(s) and respond to them according to the R.E.M.I.N.D.E.R. Exercise: Study all of the Revelation scriptures given.

Revelation

Explanation

Mysteries

Insight

Need

Demonstration

Example

Relevance

M.I.N.D. the Word Activity

"For who hath known the mind of the Lord, that he may instruct him? But we have the mind of Christ." 2 Corinthians 2:16

The M.I.N.D. the Word Activity seeks to guide your personal use of the scriptures in your daily life. It gives you the opportunity to fuse the passage's wisdom with your soul and then allow it to instruct you on the behaviors that you feel you need corrected to properly fulfill your duty to God's truth in action.

Scripture:

Motive: Why did God include it in His Bible?

Answer:

Instruction: What does God want to teach you from this passage?

Lesson:

Necessity: What about your beliefs or behaviors make this passage necessary for you?

Issue:

Duty: What must you do to observe, conform to and practice this word every day?

Change:

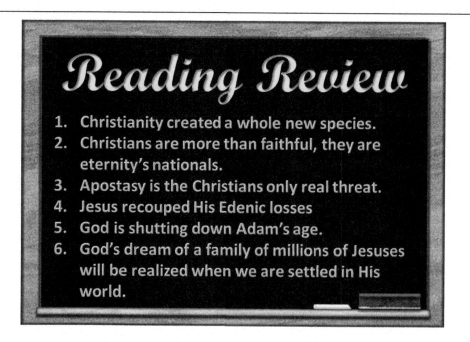

Reading Review

1. Christianity created a whole new species.
2. Christians are more than faithful, they are eternity's nationals.
3. Apostasy is the Christians only real threat.
4. Jesus recouped His Edenic losses
5. God is shutting down Adam's age.
6. God's dream of a family of millions of Jesuses will be realized when we are settled in His world.

UNIT 9

Apostolic Christians in Transition

No treatment of God's all-important New Era Apostleship Restitution campaign can begin without an extensive portrait of an Apostolic Christian. To start, this kind of Christian is inwardly restless. Though not necessarily dissatisfied with the Lord or even with His church or leaders, this saint simply craves more of God without knowing what it means or looks like. Although he or she cannot fully explain it, when the Lord answers that need, the Apostolic Christian at heart will recognize and pursue it. Until then however, these Christians are frustrated with their often unchallenging and unrewarding place in God.

Future Apostolic Christians are dutiful, so they will continue to attend and serve their churches, unless a fallout causes them to leave it. Suppressing their spiritual hunger, they nonetheless remain on the rolls in their present church because it is most likely their 'church home' where they may have been members for decades. Still, the gnawing in their souls has them doing what was once unthinkable to them; they are wandering; maybe mentally at first, but in the end, physically too.

Before becoming full fledge Apostolic Christians, these believers attend one highly prophetic or apostolic meeting after another to quench their thirst for a refreshing, and to satisfy their famished soul's cry for more of God. In this spiritual state, the astute ones refuse to blame the church or its leaders but will often chasten themselves for feeling what they feel. After all, many of them have been dutiful and fiercely loyal to their ministries for years. And for the most part, up to this point they were reasonably content with their Christianity. That is why God's sudden awakening of their apostolic roots is so disturbing to them at first. More than a few of them ignore the tug sometimes for decades, aware that it is always there in the background haunting their faith and frustrating their devotions.

Here is a question: Do you notice anything peculiar about this type of Christian? Your answer should be that most of them are seasoned believers nurtured by evangelicalism. If apostles had been plentiful in the church, theirs would be a different story. However, except for new converts that come from mature or demanding lifestyles, most of those pining for more of God today are long standing Christians. Being in the church and faithful to God for years helped them realize they are spiritually malnourished in Christ. Longevity is how they grew dissatisfied with His present messengers and messages, loyalty is why they continue to suffer through it. These people have tasted enough of the Lord to yearn for more. Their discomfort began when God abruptly unmasked an unfamiliar discontentment that keeps urging them to seek more, and it bothers many of the faithful ones.

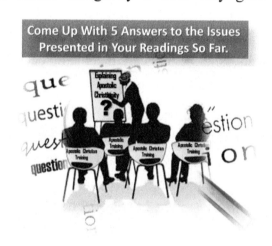

Come Up With 5 Answers to the Issues Presented in Your Readings So Far.

Hunger for what their present church cannot provide crept in and triggered disappointment about not having what they need. The answer in most cases is quite painful as it often means moving on. Apostolic folk are stable and committed members who are usually deeply entrenched their churches and ministries. So leaving their beloved Christian roots is hard on them. They know their churches and leaders will sorely feel their departure.

Since future Apostolic Christians tend to be fiercely loyal, a quality that makes them strong advocates for what the Lord wants; they will rarely badmouth their ministries or abandon their posts. These otherwise wonderful traits are ordinarily assets, but in the budding Apostolic Christian, they can be burdensome. This believer senses God's call to move on, but being dedicated and concerned about the works they will leave behind; their servant heart makes it hard for them to go. So, they suffer inwardly, grieved by the tussle between their duty and their growth. Struggling to conceal their unrelenting cravings for what is next, they find themselves becoming more and more irritated or aloof from their once cherished ministry. Habitually, duty-bound folk who love scripture, future Apostolic Christians know there is more because what God shows them in His word is nowhere to be found in their present world.

Through their devotions, Apostolic Christians gradually recognize the changes in their prayers and worship. There is more fire, fervency, and power. It is new but confusing and there is no one in their present Christian community to explain what is happening to them. Long before they are willing to admit that something new is happening, these believers are repeatedly stunned by God's subtle but persistent changes in their devotions. He is different they know, but what does that difference mean. Often it takes months, if not years for these people to accept that the Lord is calling them to a higher place in Him. The more they peer into the apostolic and prophetic, the more insistent the call gets.

As time goes on, they find they feel more at home in this stream than they ever did in the one that they are in at present. Now another nagging discomfort begins, its name is guilt. If the apostolic bound person ever thinks seriously about moving up in God, a weighty guilt overcomes them making them feel disloyal to their Christian heritage and its traditions. Even so, the restlessness continues as they work hard to conceal it by digging deeper into the church and doing more and more to silence it. Little helps to ease the discomfort or to calm the restlessness as the call to come up deepens. Search the Word of God for scripture examples of what was just discussed.

Despite learning, some of the most exhilarating things about God that they have heard in years when they frequent apostolic meetings, a perplexity sets in when Apostolic Christians at heart begin to wonder how they missed it before. These believers question their past as they contemplate their future. How is it they never heard such teachings where they worshipped for so long? Why were

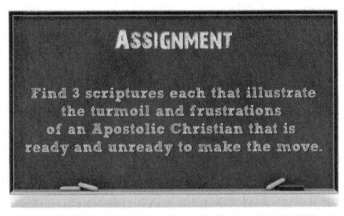

ASSIGNMENT

Find 3 scriptures each that illustrate the turmoil and frustrations of an Apostolic Christian that is ready and unready to make the move.

they not aware that they should have been hearing them all along? Doubts about the genuineness of their faith set in as the old anointing struggles with new revelations. This is normal, so keep pressing forward.

The concerns that come from hearing apostleship's wisdom for the first time are kind of the way it was with the Lord Jesus Christ. The people that were called to Him heard Him differently than those that opposed Him. His proponents said He taught with authority in ways their orthodox leaders never did. His opponents criticized His every word. What is it that Jesus provided? He gave them long overdue, in depth, and very practical answers. He fed them clear definitions, and imparted to them profound wisdom and intelligence. Jesus the Apostle of our Profession, Hebrews 3:1, made God and their faith make sense to them. That is something

Apostolic Christians yearn for most of all, for God to make sense. This is especially so if the person is highly educated and accomplished outside of the church. You are probably there already. Still, you find it frightening as the Lord keeps urging you to make your move. You fear a great part of your life is coming to an end and that is not easy to reconcile.

Connect Matthew 16:16; John 1:41; John 20:31; John 6:68; Mark 8:9; and Hebrews 3:1 to all that you just read to make strong Bible connections that strengthen and promote Apostolic Christianity.

GROUP Discussion

Making Strong Bible Connections

1. _____
2. _____
3. _____
4. _____
5. _____
6. _____
7. _____

Surrendering to the Call, Making the Move

After long prayerful nights, unsatisfactory Sunday services, and insatiable hunger have all done their jobs, the Apostolic Christian in the making, finally moves. At last, the decision to cut ties and move up in God is made and the saint dives into apostleship's deeper waters. That should be the end and the beginning of it all, right? The answer is no. It is all just beginning for this faithful, thoroughly indoctrinated, utterly baptized in tradition saint. The work is just beginning as the old wine gives way to the new. The new wineskin struggles to replace the old, and the old garment fights off the new one. The transition requires all of this to settle the newcomer into apostleship. The new world, occasionally visited before as a refresher, now seems different. It is

Share with your group how much of this you are already experiencing and what the Lord has you doing about it. It if is not you, comment on what you just read to benefit others.

demanding though it remains glorious. Still, those who enter it must get past its opposers to see and experience its truth and be fully discipled. Respond to the chalkboard question and then read on to learn the early effects of Apostolic Transitions.

Early Effects of Apostolic Transitions

The early days of a transition to apostleship should make things better but often makes them worse at first. Before discussing that, let us look at the other candidate for Apostolic Christianity. This is the one that did everything stated above, but yielded different results. Perhaps being unable to take another Sunday of the last ten to twenty or so years of their walk with Christ, this person became fed up and left, probably without cutting ties with their once

beloved church and ministers very well. Maybe it was because what was going on inside them was not clearly articulated or compassionately understood. As a result, this conventional Christian is sitting on the outskirts of God's camp. As an angry saint, this inwardly Apostolic Christian is at home every Sunday drying up inside; instead of doing what he or she did best, which was serve the Lord with gladness of heart.

Have your class work out some ideas they have for implementing the training in your organization and in their world.

Reading books, searching the web, or tuning in to Christian media just to get a bite of something worthwhile in God, they curl up within themselves waiting for the Lord to fix things for them. Your apostolic hunger never really went away. It was just upstaged by the anger or hurt you feel at how were left things with your other ministry, or with how the ministry reacted to their departure. In this instance, the person's willingness to act was good; how he or she acted on the call to Christ's apostleship became an obstacle. When they should be going forward in their calling, they are standing still, more bound than they were before.

Willing to return to Christ's fold, the isolated Apostolic Christian cannot find the right church in the beginning. In addition, connecting with the right message, the one that has the apostolic answers sought, is equally difficult. For a while, it seems the quest goes on, and on, and on for some time. That is, until they bond with the apostle the Lord appointed for them. Then things come alive again. The answers in the messages spark renewed joy and enthusiasm. They challenge and rekindle the servant's heart and zeal you once had. The power of God and His interactions during your early devotions revive and fill you with revived hope. The migrating Apostolic Christian has found a home. To repeat, that should be the end of it; right? No, it is not, and here being the reason why. Do you remember those admirable attributes listed above that qualify you to become an Apostolic Christian? Well, as customarily positive as they are in other environments, there is a downside to them that only shows up when you enter the world of apostleship. Before digging into the them, do the next exercise and then continue your reading.

Recognizing It Today

Give 3 Present Day Examples of What You Just Read Before Continuing Your Study.

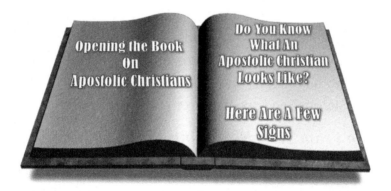

Nature of Authentic Apostleship

Here is why coming over to apostleship is not the end, and can have a rocky beginning. You see apostleship is an institutional, foundational, and ambassadorial order that is eternally structured. Its model has not been present in the church for a long time, and most likely hardly known to this generation. Most can agree that it has not been practiced much in mainstream churches, if at all. Consequently, many Christians, especially some evangelical ones, are accustomed to a completely independent faith walk. For some of them church is little more than a gathering place to snack on God's word and enjoy the company of Christians like themselves.

Coming from this background, if you are like many traditional Christians, you may believe you want apostles over you until you encounter one for real. After experiencing apostleship's kingdom structure and governance, you may feel the apostle too rigid or legalistic for your taste. Your idea of a good spiritual church or religious leader may be a coddling baby sitter and indulgent parent, but you could not know that until you encountered an apostle. Then you wonder if you are really ready for this degree of kingdom development. Now you begin ask yourself if perhaps you moved too quickly. Maybe a new pastor is actually what you craved all along.

You see, apostleship is all about kingdom and Jesus' kingship. It is not designed to confine itself to local church or personalized Christian experiences. If you stay with your decision and do not flee as some newcomers do, you may come to some telling realizations about yourself. For instance, as you settle in, you may discover that you welcome rules at work more than at church, and that could the source of your discomfort. It could also be that you want a leader that lets you lead because you may not particularly want to be led. These may be real discoveries that coming under apostleship unearth. They do not however have to become hindrances to your growth in God or your respect for apostles and apostleship.

Seeing Apostleship From Your New Wine, Wineskin and Garment

Contemporary culture has convinced many Christians to believe that when it comes to their faith, they are completely in charge. Pop doctrine suggests that Christians really do not need to be told how to practice their faith; they need only to follow their hearts. In most cases, church leaders are mainly resorted to for spiritual advice, uplifting sermons, and positive affirmation. When it comes to discipline, correction, and how to serve and behave in Christ, these concerns are exclusively the worshippers' and the Lord's business. It is neither the church's concern, nor the pastor's. It is further believed that real success in the Lord cannot be trusted to a preacher, so why allow them to impose their beliefs on you. The prevailing attitude is to let the Lord take care of the soul and let His worshipper approve or disapprove how He does it. The number one source of this judgment is what bears witness to what is in the saint's heart. If you do turn to a pastor, it should only be when your heart aches, your dreams fail, and your desires are delayed. In short, crises are the only reasons to put one's faith in a Christian leader.

Apostles are poor candidates for this type of Christian. They are leaders; take charge ministers, with God's purposes and ideals at heart. They answered their calling to fulfill His will, not the will of those they lead. Also, the very misconceptions believers have of God and His church are why He revives apostleship in the first place, so your defenses and demands will be met with resistance by true apostles. Apostleship rests on 2 Corinthians 10:8; 13:10; Hebrews 13:17 So apostles, the sincere ones, are duty bound to do things God's way. They believe that what He outlined for them as kingdom leadership in His word is what they are to follow. That face-to-face encounter that inducted them into His service is the principal reason why pastors, as modern church crises indicate, seem to see nurturing God's people differently from apostles.

Many believers' idea of a spiritual leader is a strong charismatic pastor, not a fully persuaded Christ centered apostle. Your transition to apostleship most likely imagined a spiritual connection that functioned more like a partnership rather than kingdom leadership. Modern Christianity has become too democratic for God and so He is raising up and dispatching apostles to bring the sincere saint back under His theocracy. The obstacle that is standing in His way is conventional Christianity. It primed you to expect, maybe even demand, an equality that makes you the shot-caller that affirms the pastor. When differences arise between you, you are there to remind him or her that it is your support and cooperation that sustains the work. You have demands and conditions that you want met (and kept) if you are to stay with the apostle's ministry. The problem is the apostle already has a commander and chief pulling his or her strings from the inside. The one that called the apostle as His messenger has a strong grip on this servant's soul. It tightens, sometimes painfully, every time you pit the two of them against each other. Paul in scripture called it a constraint. As loving as God's constraint may be, it is nonetheless a steely grip that genuine apostles find hard to break.

GROUP
Discussion

Session

How Does It Work?

Spend time as a group imagining how you would recognize the signs of apostleship in action from what you just read.

The apostle who is dedicated to Jesus Christ comes under attack all the time, which is why many of them anticipate your confusion, and sadly your condemnations. Experience has taught this unwavering soldier that if members like you get displeased they will leave, and the apostle will have to relive a familiar cycle. It has happened before and the signs of it happening again

are as vivid in the apostle's mind as the scars from the last time it happened are in their souls. The wounds never really heal because they are too deeply embedded in the heart, and constantly reopened when the cycle repeats itself. Nonetheless, the only thing the apostle can do about it is ride out your

reenactment one more time. A repetitive cycle such as this takes a toll on apostles' ministry. It triggers a backlash that those who walk away never consider, or maybe they deliberately count on it. Whichever it is, that cycle is why the ministry continually has to fight for credibility and stability.

Democratic church backlash is the reason many apostles' work seems small, their funds low, and their confirming accolades almost nonexistent. This very cycle is a major part of the warfare apostleship battles. It is a painful vetting that demands that God's apostles prove they are worthy of the office. Often the fallout starts with cries of legalism, shouts of religiosity, and charges of cultism. These are at the heart of some of the many pitiful sounding, sometimes unfounded (or exaggerated), church hurt stories that keep apostles restarting their works at ground zero. Following each episode, they must pick up the pieces and begin all over, and over again, because God will not let them quit. Much of it happens because Christians transitioning to apostleship fail to grasp the vast difference between them and the pastors they left behind, and perhaps previously controlled. The onslaught can go on and on until a sufficient number of Apostolic Christians joins the apostle's ministry, or rise up in it to outnumber the adversaries of the work.

From what you read above, it is easy to gather why the devoted apostle is not at liberty to indulge you or to accommodate your demands. The apostle is God's thronal official and divine order is a top priority. In this servant's world, leadership prevails, and the apostle will be the one doing the leading. There will be love and kindness for the flock, but it will not take precedence over the apostle's love for God and Christ.

You see, the excruciating humiliation the Lord uses to summon and groom His apostles teaches them to fear Him more than they fear you, because He accesses and leashes them in places you cannot reach. In spite of the hurt that some new Apostolic Christians inflict, the angry tantrums they throw, and the severe persecutions they spark, the Lord uses it all to get His apostles equipped to stand for Him. When the unpleasant seasons do occur, His power within them neutralizes it all. The truth is apostles live in the grip of the proverbial "rock and hard" place where Jesus is the rock and the threat of His retaliation the hard place. Now before you fall back on your classic "God is love" doctrine, read what the Lord says about Himself in the following passages of scripture and write your impression of them below.

Suggested Activity: Read over the following passages of scripture to get a richer understanding of God's character and justify His being a loving God nonetheless.

1. **Deuteronomy 8:2-6**
2. **Hebrews 12:29**
3. **Romans 11:22**
4. **1 Corinthians 10-12**
5. **Leviticus 20:10**
6. **1 Peter 1:15, 16**

What It Says & Means To Me

1) _____

2) _____

3) _____

4) _____

5) _____

6) _____

7) _____

9) _____

God is a Legalist

All that has been said so far shows God to be a legalist and He is not ashamed of it. For God to be a lawbreaker, He must first have been the lawmaker and that is who He is. The Lord's earthly lawmaking and lawgiving goes all the way back to the Garden of Eden, officially resumes with Abraham and culminates with Moses, and is royalized in David. As Alpha and Omega, it falls to the Creator to set up systems of government to rule His handiwork. That duty is what makes Him the judge of all, not just a single dimensional object of worship. He may be your personal Savior, but it is not for you to personalize Him to suit your

preferences and spiritual ideals. God is law, and law is God. It is impossible to separate the two. He is the Lawgiver that delegated His legal responsibilities to His Son Jesus Christ, who in turn handed it over to His apostles. The apostles then assigned the custody of God's laws to His church.

When it comes to the law or grace, or works or faith conflicts, here are some balancers you should keep in mind. God is merciful but He is also a just God. He is loving but holy too. He is forgiving and righteous, yet says He will by no means acquit the wicked. The attributes can go on, but you get the idea. Our God is all and all, and in all. Everything is in Him, is due to Him, and as Paul says to the Colossians, is for Him. He is the judge of all, beginning with judging the "thoughts and intents" of our hearts.

All that was just said is music to the ears of the righteous but irksome to the marginals. These are the people who cry foul when their "sins find them out." They repudiate God's righteousness by declaring it *legalism* as if Isaiah 9:7-9; 33:22, and James 4:12 do not exist. However, here is the way it really is with God the legalist. Legality is an outgrowth of lawmaking. Laws are essential to government. Wherever government exists, it is because laws established it. To do away with laws is to do away with government altogether. To abolish government is to eradicate legality (another form of the word <u>legalism</u>). If that happens, what takes its place is lawlessness, which is the destruction of any people. The next time you shout *legalism* to defend some disagreeable action or practice, think about what you are really saying. Stop here for a moment to read the referred to passages to understand how ludicrous it is to vacate God's law to exploit His grace. Share some thoughts with your study group on how they speak to you as a budding or settling Apostolic Christian.

As it is with the word *legalism*, so it is with the word *religious*. This term too is flung at God's

Focus List Your Main Discussion Points below.

God, the Lawgiver

1. Isaiah 9:7-9

2. Isiah 33:22

3. James 4:12

Spend time talking about what you just learned. Exchange thoughts on it and offer some ideas on how to put it to use in your world.

leaders any time order or structure is imposed on some modern saints. Efforts to obey God's word and do what is pleasing to Christ and upholding to His kingdom are met with scorn and bitter resentment. Bordering on childishness, offended saints sneer at what they call being religious. Modesty, holiness, and sanctification are met with similar disdain. Such reactions and the negative behavior that manifests them are the result of long-term carnal teaching and misapplied scripture. As stewards of the Lord's mysteries, apostles have an obligation to the

The Apostleship Difference in Churches

- Kingship of Christ
- Kingdom of God and Christ
- Sovereignty Plus Salvation
- Eternity in the Now
- Power of the Ages to Come
- Wisdom Not Just Work
- Salvation and Sanctification
- New Creation Over World Culture
- Word That Witnesses

Dr. Paula A. Price, PhD. © 2012-2014. Respectively & Inclusively — All Rights Reserved

Lord to do things His way, because not to do so is to void their commissions. That means, He ceases to back them or cover their works and leaves it up to the person or entity they obey to take His place, or take up His cause. Consider the account of Saul and the distressing spirit that replaced the Holy Spirit when Saul disobeyed Yahweh. You may not see this as a bad thing until God's snubbing the apostle's ministry spills over into your life crises. Then you and yours will also feel the Lord's disapproval.

Apostles Duty to the Lord's Righteousness

Duty to God's righteousness comes from a special insight the Lord gives His apostles into the spirit and letter of His word. They understand the context in which God judges His people and His kingdom. Apostles know for instance that the word <u>judge</u> that has become the catchall phrase for sin's self-defense, has no less than seven to ten or so different applications. While it is altogether translated judge or judgment (including judging), the truth is not all of the ways it is used are the same. Modern scripture uses the same English word judge to describe criticizing, condemning, criminalizing, opinionating, deliberating, and deciding. With these, it is also used to identify thinking and concluding, even deducing, and discriminating (meaning, to sort through). And that is in the New Testament. The Old Testament adds another string of synonyms that go from law and government to justice and righteousness, to thoughts and opinions.

All of these variations are simply called in scripture judge, judgment, and judging. The single term often refers to legal judging, trial judging, inspector judging, and culture and community judging. What you must know from this is that what you label religious or legalistic to defend your carnal human actions, make sure that: a) your claim is accurate and b) that you are not condemning God's governance in the process of challenging leadership. So how does this relate to you becoming an Apostolic Christian? It says that you are to expect different rules because apostles are guided by different criteria as predominantly kingdom ministers and not just ecclesial ones. Take a moment and jot down what you want to really remember from what you just read. Make sure it is something you want to share with others when you tell them about Apostolic Christians. This could be a good discipleship reminder later.

No.	Point to Discuss	What to Remember

For comparative purposes, look at it this way. When it comes to classifying apostles as leaders, you should expect to encounter more of a senior leader than a middle or entry-level one when it comes to interacting with them directly. Besides that, you should know if your apostle fits the presidential (for the sake of reference), the chief executive, or chairman category of divine leadership. These are not matters you should assume; you should get a revelation from the Lord on them because they determine how well you adjust to your new life as an Apostolic Christian. It is further important that you resolve these questions because they go to the heart of your destiny and decide whether or not it will be fulfilled thirty, sixty, or one hundredfold. The degree to which you resist your leaders is the same degree with which you will miss the mark in God's call on your life. After listing some things this information means to you, go on to read what you can expect from an apostle's ministry.

What You Can Expect from an Apostle's Ministry

Here is what you can expect when you enter a bona fide apostle's world. Apostles are the head of their organizations, which are formed more as embassies (apostolates) than local churches. God designed it that way even if sometimes modern Christianity is loathed to accept it. Apostles are team builders and team employers. They will apportion the delegable parts of their commissions to capable members of their works. That means you will receive aid more

often from the apostles' ministers than you will from the apostle personally, and let that be okay with you. Delegation is to be expected and actual Apostolic Christians applaud it the way the centurion did when he sent word to Jesus not come to heal his servant personally, but to, just send His word. The parable is a good leadership lesson on

delegation about comparable leaders recognizing each other's authority and scope of control. In the apostle's mind, it is better to cover all bases well than to concentrate on a few and appear to play favorites.

Another point is that the pastor may visit hospitals and jails personally; the apostle will usually send someone. Apostle's strong sense of divine order wants every member of the team to do his or her part at <u>every</u> level. The pastor may take calls from sheep directly all day, your apostle may route them to a single point of contact to be more efficient. The pastor may be fine spending days on end counseling; the apostle will often set up a counseling department to handle this responsibility. Apostles know dedicated staffers give the best and promptest service, so they delegate. The pastor may choose to attend every family's gathering; the apostle may send a representative or a gift as a token. The pastor's ministry is likely to have a single focal point; the apostle's commission is likely to be multifaceted.

Apostles' range of duties and responsibilities consist of the ministry of the word, the teaching of the flock, training leaders who in turn teach their bodies, and interaction with the commission's kingdom and ecclesial partners. These include allies, collaborators, peers, and colleagues near and far. And, you should not overlook the spiritual warfare, revelatory dispensations, and apocalyptic prophecy the apostle must be available to God to receive. Also, there is the institutional and constitutional work of apostleship that those who take it seriously undertake. Diligent apostles undertake extensive kingdom tasks to assure their commissions and its agencies remain productive and prosperous. All of these decisions have to do with efficiency and availability to God; they do not necessarily indicate superiority on the diligent apostle's part. As you can see, you will have to make some significant mental and attitudinal adjustments when you enter the commissioned apostle's world, to thrive as an Apostolic Christian in the 21st century. This is the end of this training, now you get to pass it on, but how do you do it. Take a moment now to list the things from what you have learned so far that you will use to build your Apostolic Christianity. Pick up your readings again on how to pass this on apostolically to those you lead and serve.

Suggested Activity: Read over the following passages of scripture to get a richer understanding of God's character and to justify His still being a loving God.

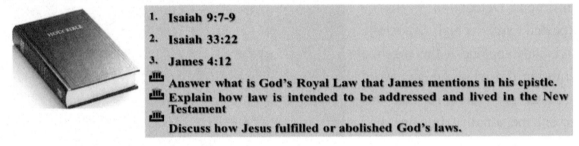

1. **Isaiah 9:7-9**

2. **Isaiah 33:22**

3. **James 4:12**

　 Answer what is God's Royal Law that James mentions in his epistle.
　 Explain how law is intended to be addressed and lived in the New Testament
　 Discuss how Jesus fulfilled or abolished God's laws.

How I Will Disciple Apostolic Christians?

After the Training Action Items

In taking Discipling Apostolic Christians to the Lord's kingdom and churches, you should know that all knowledge is passed along to achieve specific ends. Those ends come from predefined goals and objectives, which should be laid out in the beginning before you set out to communicate what you learn to others. God's aims for this discipleship program include converting, enlarging, maturing, and stabilizing His people on earth. Successfully accomplishing these aims is not incidental, it is the deliberate fruit of thoughtful planning. While enthusiasm is enough to share what you learn with close friends and family, formally transferring any kind of knowledge requires structure and order. That is what the after training exercises will help you do. They will help you organize your thoughts, plan your approach, and communicate persuasively. If you hope to be good at discipling Apostolic Christians, you should know that nothing less than meticulous planning will get the job done.

What you have just finished studying should be used and passed on, but it should be passed on in a way that yields God's fruit and not just display your knowledge. More than what you discovered about Apostolic Christianity is the point; what it takes people to believe what you say and convert to apostleship is the ultimate goal. So be good at planning and you will be great as discipling Apostolic Christians.

Action: Complete the blackboard exercise by coming with nine things you feel will be helpful to you in your effort to disciple Christians. To make interesting, come up with an acronym for your 9 Step Program. Include a comfortable but useful coaching piece in your plan. Give it a try. See if you can come up with a relevant and yet catchy acronym for the word apostolic.

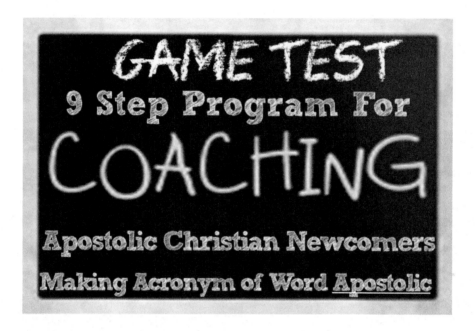

Don't Forget the Kids

If it has already been shown that the congregants and members can get left behind in the shift to apostleship, how much more their children. Ask yourself how often your plans for transitioning your organization considered your youngsters, youth, and teens? Maybe the adolescents got to sit in on some classes, but have you thought of adapting your transition plan to include bringing the whole youth department along in your changes? Most ministries do not, although their Sunday Schools may cover the names of the apostles and what they did in scripture. It is not often that transitioning apostles' whole organization is taught about apostleship today and what they can gain from them.

Typically, the apostle goes to the meetings, conferences, classes, and some coaching and returns to the church announcing it is now apostolic. Usually, the people go along at first, unsure what it means or how it will affect them in the future. Although, there are likely to be some thoughtful ones who wonder, occasionally out loud even, what it means to their faith and family. These people need to be consoled quickly so they do not stir up the church and scare the membership with imaginations and panic.

If their kids are still learning what is being replaced, they will clash with their parents at home and to keep peace the parents may just go to another church where their children are settled in what they know. So, remember the kids. Instruct your youth ministers to adapt what you are teaching the adults to every level of child in your youth group. Oh, and tell them to make it fun. Instruct them to use lots of games and activities that fit their age groups.

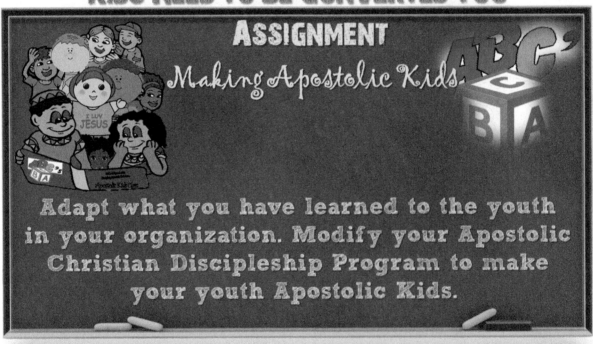

Passing It On

Okay, you now have a good deal of insight and answers on apostleship. Not to mention, with it a good amount of instruction on becoming and remaining an Apostolic Christian. So what is next? What do you do with all that you now know? Eventually, you will go out and disciple Apostolic Christians since you are well on your way to becoming one. If you are serious about being a true discipler of Apostolic Christianity, beyond casually sharing what you learned with friends, a good amount of forethought is needed. To start, you need to outline ways to interest others in this discipleship program. Next, you want to lay out how to present it in an orderly and engaging way. From there, you want to identify the best candidates for what you want to say. Remember in the beginning I said this is admittedly not for everyone, so do not force it on those for whom it is not. However, if you are in an apostleship church, it is for you; although, some of your members may not have any clue about apostleship whatsoever. Here may be a good place to start passing on the course or practicing how to do so with those who took the training with you. Just make up your mind not to let it dry up inside you.

Learn the Best Ways to Disciple Apostolic Christians

Something potent should be stirring within you now that will not let you simply put your discipleship study guide away and go back to life as usual. You now have a real chance to make a powerful difference in this area of Christianity, so how do you begin. You can begin by dividing what you want to share into two sections. Organize one for formal settings and the other for informal settings. The formal setting is for teaching assignments, the informal one is for just talking about it with friends over lunch and such. Lay out how you want to tell others what you learned. If you did the assignments, you have good tools to process your training. Revisiting your completed work will help you to envision how what was taught can benefit others. Give careful thought to expressing it well enough to make sense to believers such as yourself.

The ministry of converting Christians to apostleship requires impressing other likeminded souls with what you now know and understand about being an Apostolic Christian. To appeal to them, what you share may have to be more than talked out, how it affected you may have to be shown as well. The best setting for passing on your apostolic wisdom is one where enthusiasm joins understanding and where peace abounds. Keep your environment calm but compelling. Talk about your Christian experience before, during, and after the training to share your transition process. Be frank about your reactions to it and share a few of the difficulties you had in making the shift to Apostolic Christianity. Without being pessimistic, frankly share some of the conflicts you had with realizing God's higher call on your life and what you did to overcome them.

Be Patient and Kind

Take all questions seriously, but not defensively. The idea of Apostolic Christian Discipleship is new to the Lord's people so they need time and patience to ingest it before they can adjust their thinking to it. Do not batter or scold your learners or audiences, and by all means refrain from beating them over the head with your new knowledge. Open a warm and friendly dialogue on the merits of Apostolic Christianity, and its pros and cons. Make sure to let your listeners know that you realize that this not for everyone and you are not assuming that it is. Tell them that you are simply seeking those for whom it is. Prepare notes and strategies, and anticipate responses. Gather easy to use supports for your sessions. Use your study guide, that is why you have it. Passing it on is why you were encouraged to note your answers in it. Your training guide is a  handy way to share your discipleship material with others. Taking it with you when you go to share means you can take advantage of every opportunity the Lord gives you to tell others about the joyous benefits of becoming, or being an Apostolic Christian.

Assess the Training; Share Your Feedback

The first place to begin discipling is with a training assessment. Your feedback on the training can be positive or negative. Whichever it is, remember you will eventually use the best points of your group collaboration to plan how to pass on what you learned to motivate others to become Apostolic Christians. To be thorough, you should make a case for not becoming one in anticipation of those not called to this sphere of Christianity. That way you can address their concerns and hesitancy. Bear in mind that for a new idea to become established, it takes being able to work through all sides of it. So, be prepared to be a persuasive advocate, and also to respond to your adversaries effectively.

Preparing Your Plan and Materials to Transfer Your Knowledge

Below is an outline to help you refer to and evaluate or apply what you learned now that you have finished the training. Use it to focus the way you choose to transfer the knowledge you just gained on becoming, and motivating others to become, an Apostolic Christian. Passing on what you learned takes careful planning, and it is called Knowledge Transference. It is where you formally or informally share what you learned with others. First, you plan, then you confer, after that, you review and reinforce all that you have learned and shared.

Start your knowledge transference process by completing the following activity. Gather a group of learners, teachers, trainers, and practitioners to begin the group discussion phase of your preparations. You want to include in your group all types of Christians and a few apostles and prophets. Refer back to your Focus Group, Group Discussion, and Workshop responses in your study guide to build your model. Use what you answered to prepare for your sessions and future communications. Here is a handy tool to use as a guide to plan how you will enlighten and motivate other Christians to become apostolic.

Road to Growth Becoming An Apostolic Christian

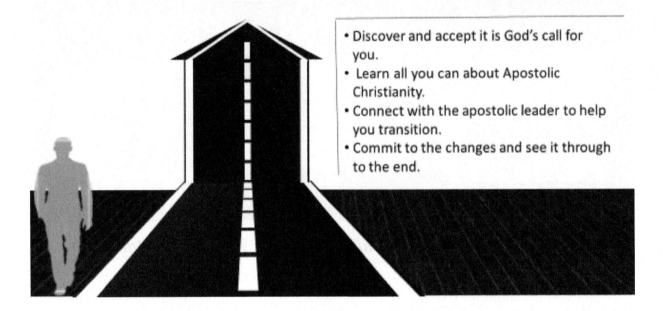

- Discover and accept it is God's call for you.
- Learn all you can about Apostolic Christianity.
- Connect with the apostolic leader to help you transition.
- Commit to the changes and see it through to the end.

My Apostolic Christian Builders

_____

_____

_____

_____

_____

_____

_____

_____

Making Apostolic Christians

FOCUS QUESTIONS

Menf

Christianity the First Civilization Teaching

How I Will Train My Leaders to Share This Teaching

HOW I WILL TRAIN MY LEADERS IN THIS

1. I will review it again myself.
   I will go over the scriptures.
2. I will write out a lesson plan.
3. I will train my leaders.
4. I will assess my leaders' knowledge.
5. I will assign my leaders to make their own lesson plans.
6. I will observe how my leaders use their lesson plans.
7. I will evaluate my leaders' teaching.
8. I will confirm the information was shared correctly.
9. I will confirm the information was Received correctly.
10. I will confirm the information was Received correctly.

Thank You for Participating

Thank you for participating in this training. By now, you are probably looking forward to using it. If you are an apostolic leader, collaborate with others like yourself to transform your organization into an apostolic one. For further guidance on discipling Apostolic Christians and on building a viable apostolic organization with them, become a part of the Lord's New Era Apostleship™ Reinstatement Campaign. The N.E.A.R. website will tell you how to do this. There you will find other teachings, resources, and apostolic leaders and members just like you to exchange ideas and strategies that support your apostleship shift.

To build on your success, do not let this be the last time you handle this material. Review it personally and with your commission team periodically to refresh yourself and to stay on track with the plan. A good deal of what you learned here can help you develop shifting to Apostleship Plans. Do not be afraid to draw on this material for it. That is why this book was written. Following these recommendations will fortify the faith you now have in Jesus Christ for multiplying and prospering His apostolic converts. Doing so will do much to increase the number of Apostolic Christians in the kingdom. Remember, apostles can only beget Christians after their own kind, something they <u>must</u> do to prosper their commissions. Once they beget them, they are to go to work transforming them into Apostolic Christians, like the ones that populated the early church. So go, make Apostolic Christians, lots and lots of them.

For more studies like this one or to deepen your knowledge of your faith and hope in our Savior, go to ppmglobalresources.com or visit the author at drpaulaaprice.com. God bless you and, happy discipling.

Helps and Tools

Information Charts for Apostles & Their Apostolic Christians

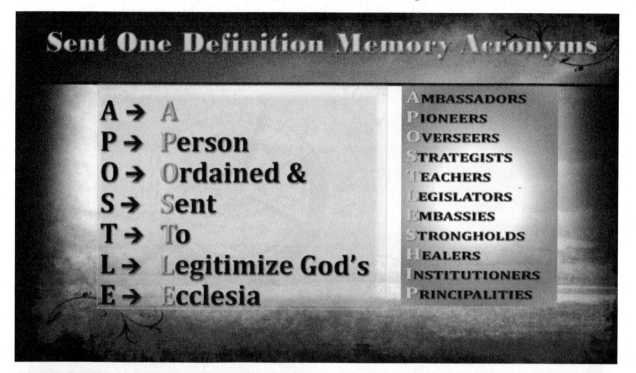

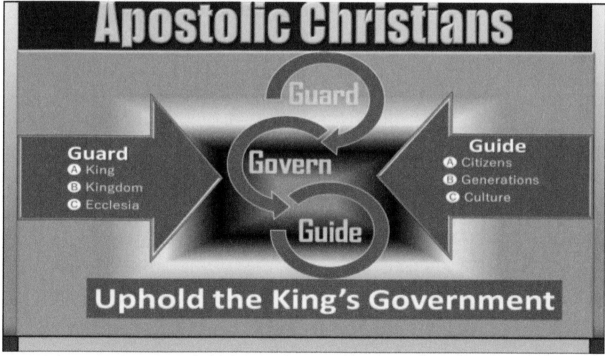

What We Mean By Apostolic Christian

1. NOT JESUS ONLY.
2. NOT THE CULTURAL CHRIST.
3. BIBLICAL APOSTLESHIP, NOT JUST APOSTOLICS.
4. SOVEREIGN SAVIOR.
5. WHOLE COUNSEL OF GOD.
6. BLENDS ALL 20+ STRANDS OF THE GOSPEL.
7. THE ORDER JESUS CHRIST BROUGHT FROM HEAVEN.
8. MODELED AFTER FIRST CHRISTIANS AND DISCIPLES OF CHRIST.
9. SCRIPTURE BASIS APOSTLES AND PROPHETS.
10. HOLY SPIRIT FILLED, LED, AND GOVERNED.
11. HOLY IN CONDUCT.
12. NOT REFLECTIVE OF DOCTRINES OF DEVILS OR HUMANS.
13. NOT SUCCUMB TO SEDUCING SPIRITS.
14. NOT MAGICAL OR MYSTICAL.
15. INCOMPATIBLE WITH WORLD CULTURES.

EPHESIANS 2:20

EPHESIANS 4:11

2 PETER 3:2

JUDE 1:7

ACTS 2:42

2 COR. 12:28

ACTS 26:18

"To open their eyes, in order to turn them from darkness to light, and from the power of Satan to God, that they may receive forgiveness of sins and an inheritance among those who are sanctified by faith that is in Me."

Separation
Education
Transformation

The Goal of

Acts 26:18

Revelation
Transformation
Sanctification

The ABC's of Apostle...

APOSTLES MOVE YOU FROM THE:
Old to New, Outer Court to Inner Court;
Discipleship to Sonship, Flesh to Spirit;
The Spirit of This World to the Spirit of
Christ.

Bearing Fruit as an Apostolic Christian

To be a productive APOSTOLIC CHRISTIAN,

You must know your place and part in your apostle's commission.

Bearing Fruit as an Apostolic Christian

To be a productive

Commission Importance

"Through him we received grace and a commission as an apostle to bring about faithful obedience among all the gentiles for the sake of his name."

Apostle Signs

"Evidence of apostleship: A sent one's fruit."

"I am free, am I not? I am an apostle, am I not? I have seen Jesus our Lord, haven't I? You are the result of my work in the Lord, aren't you? If I am not an apostle to other people, surely I am one to you, for you are the evidence of my apostolic authority from the Lord."

1 Corinthians 9:1,2. ISV

Bible Foundations

Key Scriptures:
Acts 26:18
1 Corinthians 12:28
Ephesians 2:20

Bearing Fruit as an Apostolic Christian

Paul's Commission

"I am speaking to you gentiles. Because I am an apostle to the gentiles, I magnify my ministry."
Romans 11:13

For more studies, please visit www.drpaulaaprice.com.

WE WANT YOUR FEEDBACK

Go to joinnear.com
To Give Us Your Thoughts and Ideas.

TELL US WHAT YOU THINK, WHAT YOU LIKE, WHAT YOU WANT.

About the Author

Paula A. Price is a strong and widely acknowledged international voice on the subject of apostolic and prophetic ministry. She is recognized as a modern-day apostle with a potent prophetic anointing. Active in full-time ministry since 1985, she has founded and established three churches, an apostolic and prophetic Bible institute, a publication company, consulting firm, and global collaborative network linking apostles and prophets together for the purpose of kingdom vision and ventures. Through this international ministry, she has transformed the lives of many through her wisdom and revelation of God's kingdom.

As a former sales and marketing executive, Dr. Price effectively blends ministerial and entrepreneurial applications in her ministry to enrich and empower a diverse audience with the skills and abilities to take kingdoms for the Lord Jesus Christ. A lecturer, teacher, curriculum developer and business trainer, Dr. Price globally consults Christian businesses, churches, schools and assemblies. Over a 30-year period, Dr. Price has developed a superior curriculum to train Christian ministers and professionals, particularly the apostle and the prophet. Her programs often are used in both secular and non-secular environments worldwide. Although she has written over 25 books, manuals, and other course material on the apostolic and prophetic, she is most recognized for her unique 1,600-term Prophet's Dictionary, and her concise prophetic training manual entitled The Prophet's Handbook. Other releases include The ABC's of Apostleship, a practical guide to the fundamentals of modern apostleship; Divine Order for Spiritual Dominance, a five-fold ministry tool; Eternity's Generals, an explanation of today's apostle; and When God Goes Silent: Living Life Without God's Voice.

In 2002, Dr. Price created one of the most valuable tools for Christian Ministry called the Standardized Ministry Assessment series. It is a patent pending, destiny discovery tool that tells people who they are in God, what He created them to do, and how He created them to do it. The assessment series pinpoints those called to the church, its pulpit or other ministries, and those who would better serve the Lord outside of the church.

Beside this, Dr. Price has also developed credentialing tools for ministers and professionals, commissioning criteria and practices, along with ceremony proceedings for apostles and prophets. To complement these, she designed extensive educational programs for the entire five-fold officers and their teams.

In addition to her vast experience, Dr. Price has a D.Min. and a Ph.D. in Religious Education from Word of Truth Seminary in Alabama. She is also a wife, mother of three daughters, and the grandmother of two.

The ABC's of Apostleship:

Apostleship to God and You

An Introductory Overview: Book One

$14.99 USD

The ABCs of Apostleship helps you understand apostleship from God's mind to your world. Its straightforward teaching, presents apostleship as an asset to you instead of the liability traditional theology claims it to be. ABCs is written with the Apostolic Christian in mind: *you*. You are the main one expected to explain the apostolic church you attend, or why your church is shifting to apostleship, in the workplace, restaurants, break rooms and family circles. It fills a very glaring void in the Lord's twenty or so year effort to shift His church's primary leadership to apostles. That void is your understanding of it, hence the "ABC" in the title of the series.

CPSIA information can be obtained
at www.ICGtesting.com
Printed in the USA
BVOW10s1821100816

458617BV00007B/74/P